UNLEVEL THE PLAYING FIELD

FREDERICK VALLAEYS

UNLEVEL THE PLAYING FIELD

The Biggest Mindshift in PPC History

**FOREWORD BY
GINNY MARVIN FROM GOOGLE**

MODERN MARKETING MASTERS

UNLEVEL THE PLAYING FIELD
The Biggest Mindshift in PPC History

ISBN   978-1-5445-2334-7 *Hardcover*
        978-1-5445-2333-0 *Paperback*
        978-1-5445-2332-3 *Ebook*
        978-1-5445-2335-4 *Audiobook*

CONTENTS

FOREWORD

—GINNY MARVIN, GOOGLE ADS PRODUCT LIAISON, FORMER EDITOR IN CHIEF, *SEARCH ENGINE LAND*

Over the years, Fred and I have had many conversations about the rapidly evolving role of automation in PPC advertising, some of which took place after the publication of his first book, *Digital Marketing in an AI World*. He's always been on the leading edge of understanding how to use automation to make PPC more efficient, more rewarding, and more profitable. No surprise given his background, but he's also always looking ahead in anticipation of what's to come. Fred had an early understanding of the impact machine learning is having on digital advertising.

I could not agree more with Fred that this moment requires marketers to embrace a pivotal shift in mindset. Allow me to share my personal thoughts on what makes this change so massive. It's certainly the biggest change since I started in PPC in 2005. Automation isn't new to PPC, but the exponential growth in power and application of machine learning means we're dealing with a new set of fundamentals—and a new baseline for success.

Put another way, the goalposts have shifted.

The marketers who embrace this shift and invest time to learn how machine learning does (and doesn't) work, how it's being used in PPC platforms, and which levers can now be used to inform these systems will outplay those who are still aiming for the old goalposts.

You don't need to be a computer scientist, but you do need to know machine learning fundamentals—to anticipate how an automated bidding strategy might perform, for example—to help you troubleshoot when you see results you didn't expect, and, crucially, to know how to inform the systems with your own data and insights. That's where your edge comes from— how you unlevel the playing field.

In the past, PPC marketers (myself included) were trained to be, well, control freaks in their accounts. And it paid off then. Today, be a perfectionist at your peril. Before you break out in hives, let me explain.

While machine learning algorithms can make decisions far faster and more efficiently at scale than humans can, not all of those decisions will be what we'd consider accurate. By their very nature, algorithms won't get it right 100 percent of the time, but they get it right much more often than we mortal marketers will. This can trip up marketers working with the old mindset, where every perceived bad keyword match, audience recommendation, and budget-change suggestion can sow seeds of distrust in the entire enterprise. When we expect algorithmic perfection, we're bound to muck things up and diminish the value we can bring to our accounts. That doesn't mean you should be hands-off, but when we understand the fundamentals of machine learning, we can make the algorithms work smarter for us. Mindset shift.

This is where controls play a key role. It's easy to lose sight of the fact that there are still in fact controls in an automated world that are designed to help advertisers inform the systems with their own data and insights. These are your unleveling power tools!

Bid strategy targets, seasonality adjustments, offline conversion data, first-party audience data, data exclusions, negative keywords: these are just some of the tools available to help speed up and guide the machine learning process and achieve your business goals. Further, as privacy initiatives advance and less third-party data is available, it will be critical to understand how behavior- and conversion-modeling work and what role your own first-party data can play in both targeting and measuring campaign performance.

Lastly, with this new mindset, you'll be ready to evolve your role. The value PPC marketers can bring their clients and organizations is and looks different evolving in an automated world. (It no longer looks like a Change History report filled with thousands of changes.) I, like many, rejoice that we've moved beyond spending hours crafting giant keyword lists and organizing them into exhaustively structured campaigns and then tinkering with minutiae that, frankly, often had minimal impact on overall performance. Marketers now have new opportunities to be more strategic and deliver more value.

I should note that I wrote this foreword strictly in a personal capacity. These are my own thoughts and views and not necessarily those of my employer. Nor does this represent an endorsement of any products or solutions referenced here.

I do endorse taking a clear-eyed look at automation, though. And you'll have no better guide than Fred Vallaeys and his excellent new book.

With the knowledge Fred offers up in spades here, you'll be ready to make the algorithms work smarter for you. Here's to unleveling!

INTRODUCTION

Show me a pay per click (PPC) professional who's afraid of Google AI, and I'll show you a PPC professional who already uses it to make a lot of money for their company or clients. But who's afraid of Google AI? Just about everybody.

That's because we're in the midst of the greatest mindshift in PPC history, brought about by ever-accelerating developments in artificial intelligence (AI) and machine learning (ML). Since my previous book, *Digital Marketing in an AI World*, came out, just three years ago, the landscape has already changed dramatically. Even the most talented digital-marketing professionals are finding it challenging to keep up with and understand the latest and greatest advances in PPC AI.

Help is on the way.

The AI behind Google Ads can now automate ad targeting, bidding, and even creative, delivering far better results than a few short years ago, when you were managing all this manually. But yes, it's hard to keep up. And another, equally important challenge has arisen: Google AI is taking away the advantage you used to have over your less-savvy competitors.

PPC automation has now leveled the playing field.

The results automation is delivering are good, and that's OK if you're satisfied with "good enough." But if you want to stand out—and as a marketer you know you must—you need to unlevel the playing field and beat the competition. How? By developing the ability to work with and improve upon the results available from these often-confusing automations.

Google Ads' business model is fundamentally cost-per-click (CPC). The more clicks, the more money Google makes. Its automations are designed to increase click-through rates across the board.

But at the end of the day, your business or client isn't really concerned about click-through rates. They're concerned about increasing profits and revenue and outperforming the competition. And so are you.

My last book covered why human intelligence remains essential in digital marketing, even with the arrival of machine learning. I showed that the combination of human and machine intelligence produces far better results than either can deliver on its own. A Boston Consulting Group study from 2019 found similar results and concluded, "Those that deploy ML-based technologies, with active human supervision...can boost campaign performance by...15%."

The formula is:

$$HUMANS + MACHINES > MACHINES\ ALONE$$

In the meantime, the machines have become much smarter. But the basic principle still holds true, with some variation. The new formula is:

$$HUMANS + MACHINES > MACHINES\ ALONE$$
(assisted by smart automations)   (that run complex AI automations)

What does this mean?

Having had a front-row seat at the many, successive shifts in mindset AI has caused, I know firsthand that the human factor is—and will remain—relevant, indeed essential, in digital marketing's present and future. No matter what Google says.

To unlevel the playing field, you need to shift your mindset and bring your human insight to collaborate with Google AI. You must understand where Google's machine intelligence falls short and how to build on it, by augmenting, for example, its intelligence with business insights it doesn't and can't have about your company or clients.

There are two fundamental methods for doing this. The first is to become a Google Ads power user. Learn what knobs Google already enables you to tweak, and then tweak them to your advantage. Doing this involves keeping up with what each new iteration of the technology offers.

The second method—automation layering—is less familiar to most marketers. This is supplementing Google Ads' AI-driven

PPC platform with a "layer" of your own automation that unlevels the playing field by taking your business needs—rather than Google's—into account. This may sound like a tall order to nontechnologist marketers, which is why I have written this book.

WHAT YOU'LL FIND

The book is divided into three parts. Part One, Orientation, will help you understand how rapidly evolving AI has changed the PPC landscape. You'll see why PPC automation is bringing about the biggest account-optimization mindshift in the brief but dynamic history of the field.

We'll also explore the three major challenges that we, as PPC professionals, will need to face and overcome:

1. Ad platforms will continue to automate.
2. Advertisers will have less access to data going forward.
3. Advertiser control over targeting, bidding, and messaging will keep decreasing.

In *Digital Marketing in an AI World*, I introduced three roles that humans should play in PPC marketing: Teacher, Doctor, and Pilot. These roles remain in the new landscape, but they've shifted somewhat, and you'll find out how. I'll also explore a fourth role only you can fill on the new playing field: Strategist.

The first part concludes with a close look at what automation layering is and does. We'll open the black box and look at what's inside. You'll find that Google's AI tools still leave lots of room for optimization if you know how to go about it.

I know from my experience working at Google that Google Ads is committed to helping all its advertisers place the right bid to reach the right audience with the right message. To enable this, the fundamentals—account structure, measurement, and experimentation or testing—need to be addressed with this new mindset. What has changed and what hasn't? What new approaches are now both possible and necessary? The book's second part will examine each of these fundamentals in the light of current developments.

Part Three, Implementation, will cover specific power-user and automation-layering solutions that will enable you:

- To reach the right customers with the right targeting.
- For the right price with the right bid.
- With a more compelling message and the right creative.

This is where the rubber meets the road. The learning by example and doing in this final part will help you further develop the mindset necessary to come up with your own analytical, business-oriented, and creative solutions to the challenges of a playing field that AI has and will continue to level.

ABOUT ME

When Google introduced AdWords in 2000, everything was done manually. Over time, Google layered more and more automation into the process. I saw all this happen from inside the company that invented online advertising as we know it today.

I was one of Google's first 500 employees. Working there from 2002 until 2012, I helped found AdWords, as a product specialist and then as the first AdWords Evangelist, spreading the good word about this new form of advertising.

In 2012, I went out on my own, co-founding Optmyzr, a company dedicated to enabling digital marketers to quickly extract maximum value from their PPC spend. In 2020, we hit a trifecta, winning the Global Search Awards, the US Search Awards, and the UK Search Awards for best PPC management suite. We won again in 2021. Since 2013, I've also been a regular contributor to *Search Engine Land* and *Search Engine Journal*.

When lives were upended in March 2020 at the start of the COVID-19 pandemic, I went from traveling over 100,000 miles per year to not stepping foot on a plane for eighteen months. All the conferences where I had planned to speak and educate the PPC world disappeared overnight. To continue educating and give myself a way to stay in touch with the many close friends I've made at conferences, I started the PPC Town Hall livestream (http://ppctownhall.com), a twice-a-month session where I discuss the latest goings-on in PPC with some of the brightest minds in the business. We're now at over fifty episodes, and we work hard to make the content entertaining and focused on solutions rather than theory.

I may be a technologist at heart, but I'm also keenly aware of the ongoing importance of the human factor in digital marketing. By taking a deep look at the roles PPC professionals can and will continue to play, I wrote my first book, *Digital Marketing in an AI World*, to show you that the sky, in fact, isn't falling.

Things have changed so rapidly since then that I saw the need to write another book to help you deal with PPC's increasing complexity. It incorporates the main points of the first book while focusing on cutting-edge insights into the current state of the art. It's meant to be read as a stand-alone, but if you've read the first book, thank you, and welcome back!

Above all, what you're about to read is intended to help you develop the radical new mindset that will enable you to unlevel the PPC-AI playing field. Help really is on the way!

PART FOR WHOLE

Please note that I use "Google" and "Google AI" as shorthand for PPC advertising as a whole. Why? Google is the clear leader in the PPC advertising space, with about 60 percent market share. I also have almost twenty years of professional experience with Google, which has created the template for PPC AI. Microsoft's platform is very similar, and Amazon is just now starting to build many of the same systems. With very few exceptions, the mindset and techniques you pick up here about Google Ads will be broadly applicable across these other PPC platforms.

PART 1

ORIENTATION

CHAPTER 1

·
·
·

THE THREE TRUTHS

Many PPC professionals are confused about Google Ads automation. You think you've just caught up when the next release brings a raft of new features—and takes away old features you've become accustomed to. It can be maddening.

Two things you should realize about Google AI are, first, that it has already been around for fifteen years, ever since Quality Score (QS) was introduced.

QUALITY SCORE (QS)

QS is a machine-learning system that determines the relevance of your ad to the term a customer puts into the search bar. This information helps determine the amount an advertiser pays if they get a click in the ad auction. The higher the quality score, the less they have to pay for the same position for their ad on the search results page.

Second is that AI and machine learning (ML) are not going away. Quite the contrary.

So, it's critical to understand both the rapidly evolving PPC ML landscape and the principles driving this process that will remain constant.

I call these principles the Three Truths. They can help orient you as you navigate through the AI revolution.

FIRST TRUTH: AD PLATFORMS WILL CONTINUE TO AUTOMATE

The pace of PPC AI innovation will continue to accelerate. There are at least three reasons for this.

AI will continue to advance and complexify according to the trajectory Moore's Law defines. As you probably know, Gordon Moore, co-founder and former CEO of Intel, predicted in 1965 that the number of transistors in an integrated circuit (computer chip) would double every two years, hence doubling a computer's ability to do work.

This prediction has proven correct up to the present day. And though Moore himself predicts his law will hit the barriers imposed by physical limits around the year 2025, when more transistors will no longer be able to be squeezed into the same space, it is expected new innovations like quantum computing and AI itself will continue to fuel a doubling of computing power every two years.

What this means is that hardware capacity increases exponentially. If capacity doubles every two years, it will double in two years, quadruple in four years (2^2=4), increase eightfold in six years (2^3=8), and so on.

Growth in Computing Power and Data

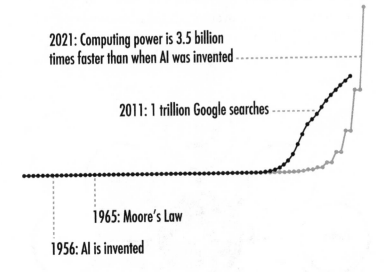

2021: Computing power is 3.5 billion times faster than when AI was invented

2011: 1 trillion Google searches

1965: Moore's Law

1956: AI is invented

Although first applied to hardware, that is, computer chips, Moore's Law has been found to be relevant to other aspects of the digital universe, like software development. In six years, AI, which is software-based, will be eight times more capable than it is now.

In other words, automation will continue to grow exponentially. Which is simply another way of saying that ad platforms like Google Ads will continue to automate PPC processes at an ever-accelerating pace.

Another relevant factor has to do with this increasing complexity. Google Ads isn't easy. To choose the right ad in real time for every search, you'd have to analyze seventy million signals, which Google AI can do in a hundred milliseconds. But this is clearly impossible for even the most prodigious quants. We just can't keep up—we're nowhere close. When my company Optmyzr makes an optimization suggestion, even for something as simple as adding a new keyword, it is often based on an analysis of over a gigabyte of data covering years of historical performance metrics.

500k+ signals on search and 70m+ on display

The third reason automation isn't going away in ad campaigns is that it works. PPC professionals like the results they get, which provides the incentive for the ad engines to build even more automation. It's a self-reinforcing loop.

Let's look at one automation, Responsive Search Ads (RSAs), to see how well-received it is.

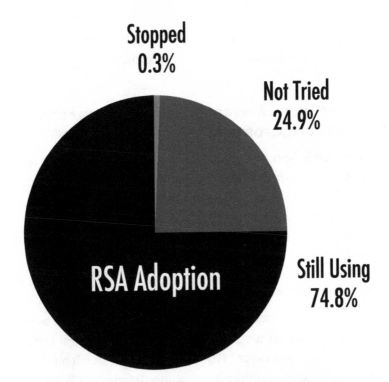

Stopped
0.3%

Not Tried
24.9%

RSA Adoption

Still Using
74.8%

Out of 4,200 accounts that tried RSAs, just 17 stopped using this automation.

Source: Optmyzr study 2020

This chart is based on Optmyzr's analysis of over 5,000 Google Ads accounts. Of the analyzed accounts, over 75 percent decided to try RSAs. Of those, only 0.03 percent decided to stop using the automation. Google automation wins in a landslide! Granted, this only tells us that advertisers keep using automations and nothing about their performance. We'll cover our findings of how RSAs perform against standard text ads in Chapter 12.

Google automation is here to stay. It will keep replacing the tasks we once did manually at an exponential rate.

SECOND TRUTH: ADVERTISERS WILL HAVE LESS ACCESS TO DATA GOING FORWARD

More data is being collected on the internet than ever before, another trend that's certain to continue. We're overwhelmed with data, both objectively and subjectively. However, you as an advertiser will have less access to this abundance of data from ad engines going forward than you had in the past.

PRIVACY REGULATION

A critical issue here is privacy. The two most prominent web privacy initiatives are the European Union's General Data Protection Regulation or GDPR—an acronym worth remembering—and the California Consumer Privacy Act (CCPA), both enacted in the last few years. These are but the tip of the iceberg: expect many more such regulations coming from various jurisdictions in the coming months and years. The trend is to limit both the data that can be extracted from internet transactions and that data's dissemination to third parties such as marketers.

Ad engines like Google are limited in how much information they can or will share with advertisers. For instance, they used to share data with advertisers about the exact words a user typed into search engines.

However, in its September 2020 update, Google Ads removed up to 70 percent of search-terms data from reports available to advertisers. Advertisers who used to manage search terms manually by scouring reports for ideas for positive and negative keywords could no longer do so at the levels they were used to.

POSITIVE AND NEGATIVE KEYWORDS

"Keyword" and "positive keyword" are basically synonyms: a keyword is a word or phrase that matches or approximates what the user would type into the search bar for your ad to be displayed. Negative keywords are words or phrases that you do NOT want to match your ads to. So, if the user's search includes your negative keyword, your ad will not be shown.

A positive keyword is simply inserted into the list of keywords for your ad: flower. A negative keyword is inserted with a negative or minus sign in front of it: -flower.

THIRD-PARTY COOKIES

Cookies are small text files a browser leaves behind on a user's device when they visit a web page. The original intent of cookies was to make the web more user-friendly, particularly by letting websites remember preferences.

There are first-party and third-party cookies. First-party cookies are those created by the website you're visiting. The fact that you're visiting a site creates a "first-party" business relationship between you and the site or company.

But many web pages rely on little snippets of code from third parties to help with common tasks like providing a way to log in or showing ads. These little pieces of code can also read and write their own cookies. Unbeknownst to many users, this means that third parties can start to collect data about them when they visit a site. Now, a user who visits a site is not only interacting with that site but also sending data to third parties whose code has been installed. While the web page may have given permission to the third party to collect this data, the user whose data is collected is usually left out of the loop and hasn't explicitly consented to this.

This leaking of data to other sites became problematic from a privacy standpoint when it started being used to track user behavior for reasons that don't benefit them directly. For example, when users add Facebook's Javascript login widget, they allow Facebook (FB) to track their actions even when they aren't interacting with FB itself.

Ubiquitous third-party cookies have created many privacy concerns. Because cookies make the web more useful, people often unconsciously accept them. But in doing so, they open the door to a lot of other activity that they may know little about and to which they haven't consented.

Privacy initiatives are doing away with third-party cookies. Apple has been first out of the gate, blocking third-party trackers from the iPhone and Safari browser as a default and launching its App Tracking Transparency Framework (ATTF), which makes apps get consent to use users' data for personalizing ads. It's possible to retain first-party cookies, but that is now at the user's, not the site's, option.

When ad networks can no longer use third-party cookies to know more about users, personalized ad targeting becomes more difficult. Google may still know what the web page someone is looking at is about and can use that to serve contextual ads. But they can no longer look at a third-party cookie to learn more about the user's other activities. This disables many advanced interest-based ad-targeting options.

Workaround responses to this issue are being developed. For instance, we'll look more closely at Google's Privacy Sandbox below.

The primary point still remains: going forward, advertisers will have less access to user data.

HEADING OFF MISINTERPRETATION

Another factor is Google's somewhat paternalistic stance toward its users, who it believes need to be protected from themselves. Google's engineers have a heightened knowledge of math and statistics, Google Ads clients often less so. Google's concern is that advertisers who are given too much data will be prone to misinterpret it. Showing less data reduces the risk of advertisers making mistakes due to misinterpretation.

An illustration of this problem is the law of small numbers. If on one day you get only one click that leads to a conversion, it's going to look like you got a hundred percent conversion rate. If you get two clicks the next day and no conversions, it looks like you've had 100 percent drop in your conversion rate. That may be true in a sense, but do you really want to make decisions based on three clicks?

Google often recommends advertisers make their automated campaigns less granular. Part of the reason for this is that it does away with small numbers. Those two clicks from before are now combined with 100 more from other ad groups, and that dramatic conversion-rate decline suddenly looks much less worrisome. Nothing has changed in the actual performance, but Google has made it less likely an advertiser will make a knee-jerk reaction that negatively impacts their campaign's future.

Numbers can be misleading in other ways. Ad position is something advertisers used to look at closely: how often your ad appears at the top of a search results page and how often it doesn't appear until the second page or later. Google used to give its advertisers an averaged position but no longer does because it was essentially meaningless. What's important isn't the position itself, but how it was arrived at.

Say you get an averaged position of 1.5. Does this mean that you're in first position half the time and in second position half the time? Or does it mean that your position is usually very good but is occasionally really bad?

Both of these lists of the position where your ad was shown average to 1.5, but they represent vastly different scenarios:

$$\frac{1+2+1+2+1+2+1+2+1+2}{10} = 1.5$$

produces the same average as:

$$\frac{1+1+1+1+1+1+1+1+1+6}{10} = 1.5$$

By not reporting average position any longer, Google prevents misinterpretation.

Sometimes meaningful data just isn't available. Machine learning is often a bit of a black box. It is applied to a mass of data and delivers often stunning results by identifying patterns humans can't see.

ML systems like neural networks achieve this by scoring nodes, much like the brain connects synapses. Except humans can explain why we arrive at certain conclusions, whereas ML can only tell us the scores for the nodes but can't translate this information into something we can make sense of. Hence, we can't ultimately determine which portions of the data led to the AI's conclusions.

THIRD TRUTH: ADVERTISER CONTROL OVER TARGETING, BIDDING, AND MESSAGING WILL KEEP DECREASING

In other words, advertiser control has decreased, and that trend will continue. The problem is that nobody likes to feel not in control.

Take a look at this photo:

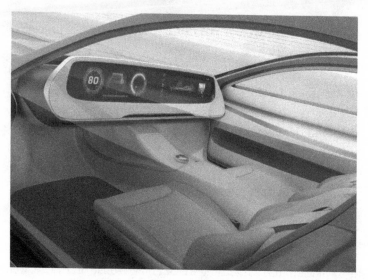

It's a mock-up of the interior designs for a self-driving car like those from Google. Very sleek and aerodynamic. The problem is what's missing: no steering wheel, no rearview mirror, no gas pedal, and no brakes. They shouldn't be necessary in a self-driving car. But very few drivers would be comfortable getting into a car that doesn't provide some option for taking over if a mistake or perceived mistake has been made. Would you?

Google Ads also tends to take control away from its advertisers. Why? Automation works better in more predictable environments with fewer variables. In particular, a feature not being used or being used incorrectly is a candidate for the chopping block, even if the feature, used properly, would have been most useful.

As an example, Google recently decided to phase out Broad Match Modified (BMM) keywords. To understand why, we need to go into the details of Google's keyword system. The following table illustrates Google's different keyword match types:

MATCH TYPE	SAMPLE KEYWORD	WHAT *CAN BE* DIFFERENT BETWEEN QUERY AND KEYWORD	WHAT *CANNOT BE* DIFFERENT BETWEEN QUERY AND KEYWORD	COULD SHOW ADS FOR SEARCHES LIKE...	BUT NOT FOR SEARCHES LIKE...
BROAD	vacation San Francisco	1) Extra words can be anywhere 2) Word order of keywords can be changed 3) Keywords may be left out	A query must still be in the same realm of what the keyword and ad are offering	a) vacation San Francisco b) vacations in SF c) ideas for vacation in San Francisco d) vacation planning for San Francisco e) summer vacations San Francisco f) day trips in the Bay Area g) Palo Alto hotels	h) jobs in San Francisco
PHRASE	"vacation San Francisco"	1) Exact words can be anywhere 2) Word order of keywords can be changed if that doesn't change the meaning 3. Close variant rules apply	Word order cannot be different if that changes the meaning, e.g., "from NY to SF" cannot march "from SF to NY"	a) vacation San Francisco b) vacations in SF c) ideas for vacation San Francisco d) vacation planning for San Francisco e) summer vacations San Francisco	f) day trips in the Bay Area g) Palo Alto hotels h) hobs in San Francisco

MATCH TYPE	SAMPLE KEYWORD	WHAT CAN BE DIFFERENT BETWEEN QUERY AND KEYWORD	WHAT CANNOT BE DIFFERENT BETWEEN QUERY AND KEYWORD	COULD SHOW ADS FOR SEARCHES LIKE...	BUT NOT FOR SEARCHES LIKE...
EXACT	[vacation San Francisco]	1. Close variant rules apply	No extra words can be in the query unless doing so doesn't change the meaning of the keyword	a) vacation San Francisco b) vacations in SF	c) ideas for vacation San Francisco d) vacation planning for San Francisco e) summer vacations San Francisco f) day trips in the Bay Area g) Palo Alto hotels h) jobs in San Francisco

A result on an exact match keyword must match what the user types in the search bar almost exactly. It's obvious that it would be tremendously limiting to only have exact match keywords. Especially since Google has determined that 15 percent of all searches are unique, making them hard for advertisers to guess and add to their accounts.

Advertisers needed a low-effort way to capture the potential of these hard-to-guess searches. That's why Broad Match keywords are useful to help advertisers show ads for all relevant queries, even the 15 percent of searches that are new and unique. The problem is that Google sometimes also shows ads for Broad Match keywords that aren't particularly relevant.

So, due to Broad Match's inherent risk of relevancy problems, advertisers started shying away from Broad Match in favor of Exact Match keywords.

Their argument: the risk of showing for irrelevant broad variations outweighed the benefit of the additional traffic. This undesirable trade-off did in fact exist in the days before auction-time bid automation—which Google calls Smart Bidding—but it's much less of an issue today. In other words, advertisers had a legitimate complaint, but they were often overreacting. (Yes, you may see traces of my old job as the AdWords Evangelist shining through here and there when I take a heavily pro-Google stance.)

SMART BIDDING

Google Smart Bidding is a form of automated bidding in which ML sets the amount of each bid at the time of each auction. This enables it to take real-time factors such as user location and time of day into consideration. Strategies include Maximize Conversions with an optional tCPA (target cost-per-acquisition) and Maximize Revenue with an optional tROAS (target return-on-ad-spend), among others.

In standard automated bidding, bids are updated on a fixed schedule, say every fifteen minutes, every hour, or daily. In between bid updates, every time the ad enters an ad auction, it gets the same bid. This means the bids are less precise than with Smart Bidding, the real-time auction-level bids of which have greater precision and accuracy.

There will be more on Smart Bidding later, in the chapter devoted to bid strategy.

But before Smart Bidding helped alleviate some of the concerns of advertisers, Google decided to launch a hack to their match types, by introducing a quasi-match type called Broad Match Modified (BMM).

One example I remember from my time at Google was trying to explain to an advertiser why we'd shown their ad targeting the keyword "Britney Spears posters"—I worked at Google a *really* long time ago—for a search for "Britney Spears."

When you sell posters, dropping the core word "posters" from the keyword understandably makes a big difference. BMM is a variation of the Broad Match keyword type that Google introduced in 2010 to address such complaints from advertisers.

To combat showing ads for irrelevant queries while still allowing for extra traffic from closely related searches, Google said advertisers could specify the words in the keyword that were *absolutely critical* by adding a "+" in front of those. In the Britney Spears example, the advertiser could create the following BMM: "Britney Spears **+poster**"

Now, an advertiser selling only Xbox video games could target a keyword like "video games for +Xbox." That way, their ad would show for searches like "**Xbox** games" but not for "**Nintendo** games."

Another example. A travel site focused on luxury vacation homes could use a keyword like "luxury vacation **+homes** in San Diego" so their ad could show for "vacation rental **homes** near La Jolla," but not for "luxury **hotels** in San Diego."

In February 2021, my company, Optmyzr, did an analysis of 162 million positive keywords. We found the following:

- Eighty-nine percent of advertisers use BMM keywords.
- Fifty-five percent of advertisers who use broad match

modified *always* put a plus in front of every term in their BMM queries, e.g., +video +games +for +Xbox.

- Ninety-five percent of all broad match modified keywords have a plus in front of *every* term of the keyword. Only 5 percent of keywords are more selective about plussing words—for instance, "video games for +Xbox."

This essentially turns Broad Match Modified into modern-day Exact Match keywords. The whole purpose of BMM, which my Britney Spears posters advertisers would have found most useful, was defeated. So, Google took BMM keywords away, eliminating a potentially important, if often misused, marketer control. Yet despite how few advertisers used the feature as intended, contributors on blogs like *Search Engine Land* were still very angry, because those of us who want to be better than average are seeing some of our controls taken away because most people didn't bother to learn how to use them correctly.

PROBLEMS AND SOLUTIONS

Google's perspective—we'll get into the reasons for it below— is that its job is to deliver the best results for the maximum number of its users and advertisers. Here's the formula:

More automation + less data + fewer controls =...drum roll please...

Advertising that works for everyone!

Say what? Yes, this is advertising that works for everyone. Unless you're a PPC expert who loves data and control.

PPC experts want to unlevel the playing field and distinguish themselves from average players. To do this, you need to be able to manipulate a complex and ever-changing system.

There are two complementary ways of going about this:

1. Become a Google Ads power user and use the controls the system continues to offer. This is what those who used BMM keywords properly were able to do.
2. Insert your own layers of automation that collaborate with Google's to achieve your real business goals by teaching the machines what your ads are really after.

This requires a major shift in mindset for how to optimize—in fact, the biggest mindshift in PPC history.

The first step in unleveling the playing field is knowing how it got leveled in the first place. So, next we'll examine how the PPC ecosystem got to where it is today and why.

GOODS AND SERVICES: E-COMMERCE AND LEAD GEN

There are two broad categories of advertiser: those who focus on e-commerce and those who focus on lead generation. The first category involves goods and the second services. For the first category, the key metric in Google Ads is return on ad spend (ROAS), which is inversely related to Amazon's advertising cost of sale (ACoS). For the second category, the key metric is cost per acquisition (CPA). While these metrics aren't identical, they are comparable.

The examples you'll find in this book tend to focus on either e-commerce or lead generation. However, it's generally quite easy to extrapolate from one to the other.

CHAPTER 2

•

•

•

•

THE AI MARKETING LANDSCAPE

When I was at Google, each team held a quarterly "team bonding" off-site. Once, this was held at our local concert venue, the Shoreline Amphitheater, across the street from the Googleplex.

Google is big on free food and other perks, so boxed lunches with sandwiches had been brought in from the Googleplex for my team. Not everyone at the Plex was attending this off-site, so admins staffed the food table, checking off names, ensuring that there'd be enough for those attending.

As I was waiting in line, I saw that Sergey Brin, Google's co-founder, was a few spots ahead of me. He was waiting patiently with the rest of us—no special skybox, no gofer to bring his food to him.

Sergey, being the boss, and not on my team, didn't have his name on the list. The hapless, recently hired admin in charge turned him away, sandwichless. He left as requested but was soon called back. One of my teammates told her, "That's Sergey Brin, the company's founder. Give the man a sandwich!"

We all had a good laugh.

To me, this incident represents the company's and its star leadership's admirable humility. It is also emblematic of the radically level playing field Google is committed to in its values and daily practice.

This company value creates a strong gravity around implementing and supporting the average advertiser. For many, average is plenty good enough. But not all of us can afford to be as unflappable as Sergey.

Remember that Google doesn't extend this evenness to its own competition. In its field, Google looms large. In creating a level playing field for its advertisers, Google has radically and profoundly unleveled and dominated the search engine ecosystem.

That's the attitude digital marketers should and can take. Here's an example of how one marketer unleveled the playing field, which we'll return to in subsequent chapters.

AUTOMATION LAYERING: CLOSING MORE MORTGAGES

Let's take an example. Betty works for a top-tier bank that sells mortgages online. The process starts with a prospective customer filling out a lead-gen form that goes into the bank's customer relationship management (CRM) system. Mortgage specialists follow up and close the loan, often with lag times of up to two months.

As the bank's digital marketing expert, Betty has always managed bids manually. But she knows she could get more from her department if they didn't have to spend so much time doing the same repetitive math, uploading their bulk changes in the Ads Editor, and then clicking "save and apply." She educates herself on Google Smart Bidding and sets up a test using a tCPA strategy.

"Conversions" go up immediately. More potential customers fill out the lead-gen form, while total ad costs remain the same. The bank's CPA is actually lower than the limit Betty set. It looks like the automated bidding system is doing exactly what it's supposed to do.

Six weeks later, when Betty has enough data to evaluate results, it doesn't look like the new strategy has been successful. Yes, more prospects are filling out the lead-gen form than ever before. But the bank is closing fewer mortgages. Google Smart Bidding is bringing in more leads, but they're of lower quality than the ones Betty got when she was managing bids manually.

Google is performing as instructed, but not delivering the desired results. But Betty doesn't conclude that Smart Bidding is broken or a bad fit for her company. Instead, she investigates.

Betty finds that Smart Bidding has been doing its job of finding more prospects who then fill out the lead-gen form on the landing page. But it hasn't accounted for the differences between good leads and bad ones. That's because her team hasn't fed Google any data about which responses to which questions on the lead-gen form are most likely to correspond with a high-quality lead. Smart Bidding has been operating with a conversion signal that's incomplete and doesn't align with the bank's true goal: to *close* mortgages, not just get leads.

Betty digs into ways of teaching Google the value of specific leads. An analyst on her team builds a simple regression model that correlates the desired outcome—a signed mortgage—to different variables captured in the bank's lead-gen form and CRM. Betty's team then automates the process of feeding these findings back into the Google Ads AI system using the conversion adjustments feature in Google Ads. This refocuses the system on finding more conversions that have a high likelihood the prospect will close a new mortgage rather than just fill out the lead-gen form.

Within a month, the bank's lead volume drops, but the number of mortgages closed goes up. The fewer lead-gen form-fills generated are of far higher quality. Betty has used her own automation to change the definition of what constitutes a conversion and combined this with Google's world-class automated bidding to get better results in less time.

This is automation layering.

Automation Layering

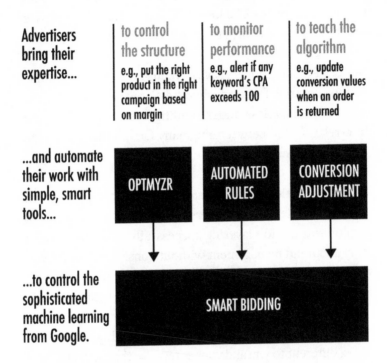

Advertisers bring their expertise...	to control the structure e.g., put the right product in the right campaign based on margin	to monitor performance e.g., alert if any keyword's CPA exceeds 100	to teach the algorithm e.g., update conversion values when an order is returned
...and automate their work with simple, smart tools...	OPTMYZR	AUTOMATED RULES	CONVERSION ADJUSTMENT
...to control the sophisticated machine learning from Google.	SMART BIDDING		

A machine only learns as well as the instructions it's given. Betty has automated and layered the parameters in her bank's mortgage-approval process with Google's state-of-the-art machine learning Smart Bidding. This sets bids that dramatically surpass the results competitors relying solely on Google AI will get. The system is now working to achieve the bank's goals, not Google's.

Betty unleveled the playing field, and so can you.

But until you understand what Google automates, you can't see what you can and should take control of yourselves. That's not a trivial problem.

Once, it was fairly simple to know which Google AdWords knobs to turn. But Google's move towards sharing less data, removing controls we've long had, and accelerating the pace of automation—the three truths—have radically changed that.

Newer PPC practitioners have never had the relatively simple manual controls featured when AdWords launched in 2001. So, there is now less understanding in the industry of the interrelationship between the many factors that determine a campaign's success.

Betty's sophisticated understanding of the interplay between bid management and conversion tracking allowed her to deploy automation layering successfully. Had she thought only about bid management without considering which conversions were meaningful, she would have continued to get subpar results. And she probably would have blamed Google.

What constitutes a "conversion" will probably mean something different to you and your enterprise than it did to Betty. The adjustments you'll need to make to Google's suite of automations will likewise be unique to your enterprise. If they were commonplace rather than unique, Google would have automated them by now.

It's in what differentiates your company that you will find the opportunities to contribute your unique insights to Google and unlevel the playing field. And, with what you're about to learn, I'm confident that you can get on top of the trends shaping AI digital marketing to meet your goals and stay ahead of the competition.

SURVEYING THE LANDSCAPE

As of the early 2020s, most Google automations are task-oriented, with little interconnection among them. Google offers Smart Bidding, close variant keywords, Responsive Search Ads, and many more—an impressive collection of automations that doesn't cohere as a suite. Each takes a single task once done manually and automates it.

Google's automations are therefore incomplete replacements for human PPC managers. They are a collection of star players who don't always function well as a team. They need a human coach who has the creativity, ingenuity, and adaptability needed to make them work together to win the game.

PPC marketers have to manage these individual automations to ensure they don't crater results due to an overlooked setting or interactions that undercut one another. Every marketer today has to adopt a new mindset and relearn their craft as it applies to these AI tools.

Let's look at how we got to where we are, and then at both the benefits of and, even more importantly, problems with the current system.

ITERATIVE UNLEVELING

Google is very explicit about its goal of leveling the playing field for advertisers. That's why it's been so successful.

In the pre-Google days, Yahoo!—the then-dominant search engine—sold only banner ads to big companies. A small local shop, for example, had no way to compete with a national retailer like Best Buy. Google deliberately structured their platform to address that inequity.

Regardless of how much an advertiser was willing to pay on a cost-per-click basis, the relevance of their ad was an equally important factor in determining its placement. Suddenly, Joe's Photo Shop could play on the same field with Sony and Best Buy. If Joe put in a bit more time to write a great ad, pick the right keyword, and optimize, he could even beat the big dogs despite his smaller budget. (Please remember Joe's Photo Shop, as we'll return to it in the following chapters.)

Unlike Yahoo!, Google didn't have a minimum spending requirement. At a time when Joe and his modest $3,000 advertising budget would have had trouble getting a traditional ad sales rep to return his calls, Google eliminated the need to contact one at all.

Advertisers no longer had to call ad sales reps and negotiate. They could just log into Google AdWords and type in their keywords, ad text, and bids. Joe could set a bid as low as a penny per click and a budget of a few dollars a day to get his ad into the auction and compete for the attention of the same buyers his competition targeted.

Letting advertisers pay just pennies per click on a CPC basis, when big brands were willing to guarantee paying much more on the traditional CPM basis—cost per "mille" or thousand impressions—was a novel idea at the time, first tried by innovative entrepreneur Bill Gross's Goto.com. Now, it's abundantly clear that this business model, which was later perfected by Google, was much better than Yahoo!'s.

But the big brands caught on, got more efficient, and started placing higher bids. AdWords grew increasingly complex and difficult enough to use that many established smaller companies got mediocre results and gave up on it.

Google's investment in AI and automated processes was driven, in part, by its commitment to helping the Joes of the world. Through almost two decades of growth, AdWords became ever more complex, and many advertisers walked away in frustration, because getting good results was too tough. Fewer advertisers competing in an auction makes the auction less competitive, which hurts Google's revenues. If they could make it easy again for the Joes of the world to take part in the ad auction, consumers would get more choices, and advertisers and Google shareholders would also benefit.

Along the way the playing field became leveled again. Now, Google Ads—as AdWords was rebranded—is so easy to use that anyone with a spreadsheet of their company's products can turn on Smart Shopping campaigns and compete with the big boys. No need to choose keywords, set bids, create ads, or worry about the nuances. Google handles it all!

SMART SHOPPING

Smart Shopping campaigns connect to your merchant feed, which contains details about all the products you sell. Smart Shopping then automatically shows users what it determines to be the relevant ad corresponding to a specific search. They are billed as complete end-to-end automations (set it and forget it) but can still be optimized through automation layering.

Most Joes are just happy to get a slice of the online sales pie. But the companies, large as well as small, that can figure out how to optimize campaigns with the new set of controls that come with increased automation can unlevel the playing field back in their favor.

GOOGLE AI

Early forms of artificial intelligence have been around since the mid-1950s. Google has become a major force in developing AI and machine learning in the twenty-first century.

Google accelerated the state of AI by over a decade when its DeepMind division spent hundreds of millions building AlphaGo, which began beating international grand masters of the board game Go in 2016. Go was much more difficult for computers to play than other games, including chess. AlphaGo's triumph is now considered a machine-learning watershed.

Google is one of the very few companies with the resources to do such "basic AI research" with potentially wide applications, including in digital marketing. As a search engine, Google also has a universe of data, both on what people search for and what their behaviors say about their interests, with which its AI system can be trained to improve which ads are shown to which users.

Increasingly, a company's value is directly tied to how much information it has about its customers. With the possible exception of Facebook and Amazon, few companies can compete with the sheer scope and vast amount of data that Google has on its search engine's users.

Every time someone initiates a search, Google already knows where they are geographically, their demographics, what they've searched for in the past, and what they're generally interested in. From all the data it's collected, Google can build a remarkably complete picture of online shoppers, interpret the searches they make, and anticipate many of their needs.

You may have read the 2012 *New York Times* article "How Companies Learn Your Secrets," which became the basis of the much-repeated story that Target knew a girl was pregnant before she herself told her parents. While the details of what Target knew and how they used it for targeting were probably overblown, the point is that even ten years ago, companies with lots of data already knew your family better than you did. Companies today have even more data and access to better machine learning, so we can only imagine what they have construed about each of us.

For example, Google AI "knows" which results to deliver to different users who have typed the search term "Odyssey." A recently married user who has been reading car reviews will be sent to the Honda site. A college student studying literature will be directed to an entry on Homer and a science-fiction movie buff to Stanley Kubrick's 2001: *A Space Odyssey*.

All users are shown fewer irrelevant results. And Honda now pays for ads directed only to those who might be in the market for a minivan. Big as it is, Honda would never be able to do this on their own. Only Google has access to as much qualifying data.

Honda, like any advertiser, can adjust bids based only on

such macro-indicators as time of day, geography, device type, gender, and age. Google Ads alone can set bids at the actual time of a search, based upon the vast amount of granular data it has access to, comprising over half a million search signals and over 70 million display signals.

FLOC

FLo...what? Federated Learning of Cohorts (FLoC) is, at the time of writing, one of Google's many new AI innovations created in response to privacy concerns. As such, it offers a glimpse of where AI is going. Let's break the term FLoC down.

Federated Learning (FL) was invented when users got concerned about voice assistants like Google Home and Alexa sending into the cloud recordings not only of their personal conversations with the devices, but sometimes also conversations not intended for the digital assistants. Formerly, the only supercomputer powerful enough to process conversational commands in real time was in the cloud.

But then Moore's Law kicked in, and mobile devices and voice assistants got enough computing power to do some of the ML processing locally. This means that a user's data no longer had to leave their house or their browser to be made useful. Overnight, your voice assistant could update itself and merge its machine-learning model anonymously with those of other users, with the resulting new model generated in the cloud getting returned to your device. The result is it can better understand you than ever before without letting the data used to build the models leave your device. I'm oversimplifying this, so check out a book on federated learning if you really want to understand how this works.

Several other initiatives to protect user data while still enabling interest-based advertising and remarketing without third-party cookies are in development, such as Microsoft's PARAKEET, and Google's TURTLEDOVE. (You'll notice that these acronyms are all riffs on the FLoC/flock pun, which you might find either clever or annoying.) How advertisers will take advantage of these new and upcoming solutions is a quickly evolving field whose "best practices" have yet to be developed.

You can expect many more AI innovations such as FLoC in the coming years. You really can't compete with Google in the AI arena, and smart advertisers won't try to. But you can and should supplement Google AI with your unique business needs and data.

GETTING GRANULAR

Let's take the example of Alonzo's Auto Parts store in Michigan. Google Ads was too complicated for Alonzo to operate without help, and his budget isn't big enough to hire a PPC agency. He wants something plug-and-play.

Alonzo turns his advertising over to Google's Smart Shopping. He gives Google a list of his products, their features and prices, and his advertising budget. Smart Shopping then decides which ads to show for which search terms, what platforms to use (YouTube, Gmail, and/or search engines) and how much to bid for each product.

For companies like Alonzo's, which would otherwise miss out on this kind of advertising, something is better than nothing. Alonzo is happy to cede control over everything except his budget because he doesn't have time to learn how Google Ads machine learning works. He's busy running his business and doesn't want the extra hassle. He just wants new customers at a reasonable price.

Winter hits. The morning after the first heavy freeze, Alonzo comes in early to prepare for all the customers who he's anticipating will need new batteries in the morning, since old batteries tend to fail with the onset of colder temperatures. But they never arrive. Smart Shopping hasn't taken today's subfreezing temperatures into account.

Alonzo would like to dedicate more of his budget and raise his bids for batteries on really cold days. But he also sells thousands of other auto parts the weather has no impact on.

Alonzo thinks that Google's Smart Shopping automations can't factor in the impact of weather. So, he leaves the system alone and misses out on an opportunity. The truth is that he could leverage the system by adding a small automation layer that basically instructs the system to raise CPC bids or set more aggressive tCPA or tROAS targets when the weather first goes below freezing in November or December.

We'll return to Alonzo and his auto parts store in later chapters to see how he turns this problem into an opportunity.

Now, let's look at the ways in which AI, without the human factor, can let you down.

·
·
·
·

CHAPTER 3

WHEN MACHINE LEARNING BREAKS DOWN

Machine learning is much better than humans at certain tasks, such as analyzing reams of data. It can even beat grand masters at both chess and Go. But there are other tasks that humans perform much better than machines: ones that involve context, nuance, and creativity.

CONTEXT

Many of the automated tools we now rely on are narrow in scope and uncoordinated with other, related tools. They then make some stupid choices that a human-run system wouldn't.

Say an automated bidding rule notices a sudden decline in conversion rates and decreases the bids for the keywords involved. On the surface, that sounds right. It's exactly what we expect. The system's job is to make predictions about future conversion rates to help set sensible bids for ads in future auctions. But without context, this can go wrong fast.

What if the conversion rate dropped, not because users became less interested in the advertiser's offer, but because the website had technical issues and took too long to load? A 2017 Akamai study showed that a two-second increase in page-load time doubles the bounce rate.

If conversion rates decline because of a landing-page technical issue, is the right action to reduce bids and hope things get better? Or would it have been better to notify the advertiser that they should fix their landing page? I've seen real-life examples where bids were reduced for this reason and were kept low long after the landing pages were fixed. The advertisers' sales declined unnecessarily.

Machine learning, by its nature, is bad at answering "why." It can reliably identify a picture of a cat. But it can't tell you why it's a picture of a cat and not a dog. Humans are adept at contextualization. They can't analyze nearly as much data as an ML system. But they are much better at explaining how things fit together in the bigger picture. They can explain why what's shown in the picture is a cat.

Take another example. At Optmyzr we created an ML model to predict which trial sign-ups would convert into subscribers of our software. As with most software sales that involve free trials, the majority of users won't convert after their trial ends, so we found it easy to write a prediction system with high accuracy.

The problem was that the system tended to predict most users would *not* convert. That's safe enough, since again most users don't convert.

In other words, if 90 percent of users have not converted historically, a prediction mechanism that guesses every single trial user won't convert will be right 90 percent of the time. A 90 percent prediction accuracy sounds amazing. Except this calculation is completely useless because it doesn't provide the context needed to help my team know which users are more likely to become ongoing customers and therefore are worthwhile to spend more time with.

Another, less accurate algorithm that attempts to predict the 10 percent of users who will eventually convert would be much more useful. In other words, with a sample of a hundred trial users, it's much more useful to get twenty predictions of likely conversions, even if half of the predictions are wrong, than it is to get a model that predicts nobody will convert and is 90 percent accurate in doing so.

An example from my time at Google will help explain.

DRAWING THE LINE

Google hired me in 2002 as an AdWords specialist to review new ads as they came into the bin (that's what we called the ad-approval system) and ensure they were relevant, family-safe, and followed policy guidelines. This was a new initiative. Google previously hadn't exerted much control over ad content. Instead, it had allowed advertisers to run what they wanted. It then used the public as auditors, taking down an ad if it brought in too many complaints.

This policy worked fine until AOL came on as Google's first major syndication partner. As part of the deal, Google agreed to review all advertising for pornographic content. While porn ads were allowed, we didn't want to show these for nonpornographic keywords and risk delivering off-color content to users not looking for it.

Google went on a hiring spree, bringing in people like me even before they had a place to put us. We ended up in the "I'm Feeling Lucky" lobby conference room—a reference to Google's early days, when in submitting a search, you could punch the "I'm Feeling Lucky" button and be taken straight to the highest-ranked organic result. It's one of the features that helped launch Google successfully in search, although it eventually became irrelevant and was discontinued.

My colleagues and I spent all day every day reviewing ads. Well almost all day—I did make it a point to gear up for the company's twice-a-week pickup roller hockey game in the parking lot. Sergey was usually there too, although Larry had stopped playing before I joined. So here we were playing pickup hockey with one of the soon-to-be richest people in the world. And then we busted the rearview mirror of a car belonging to someone at another company. Google hadn't gone public yet. Most of us were young and spent all our money on tech gadgets or going out, so we were all worried about how much it was going to cost to fix.

But back to the ad bin. We each reviewed about a thousand ads a day, marking each "family safe," "non-family safe," or "adult." Millions of dollars in potential revenue were at stake if we violated the AOL contract. We knew that if we made a mistake and something pornographic showed up on AOL, we'd quickly be shown the door, and, worst of all, lose all our chances at getting pre-IPO stock in one of the Valley's hottest startups at the time.

Like most of the others working the bin, I often didn't feel so lucky. Every Friday, someone from HR would come into the conference room and ask unfortunate colleagues to clear their desks. Not that there was much on those desks to clear, considering we were crammed in shoulder to shoulder. But I, like most of my compatriots working in the bin, used to have nightmares about it!

I'm originally from Belgium. When Google decided to further expand AdWords in the Western European market, I started translating Google AdWords into Dutch. My job involved reviewing ads, which meant making sure Dutch porn stayed out of the hands of the average user.

To ensure Dutch speakers looking for porn were able to find it, but those who weren't didn't do so accidentally, Google's engineers used early versions of ML to create a list of likely pornographic search terms in Dutch, ranked on a confidence scale from 0 to 100 percent. The engineer who built the system printed out and gave me that list. My job was to determine at what point a search term went from "potentially not pornographic" to "definitely pornographic."

I literally drew the line. I marked the spot between two search terms, setting a threshold. Search terms ranked above the "definitely pornographic" line could return pornographic ads on the theory that anyone using those keywords was trying to find exactly that.

That's how machine learning often still works in search. The machine scores a list of search terms. A person—not the machine—then draws a line, setting a threshold beyond which certain results are or aren't allowed to be shown. The list of terms is ranked in a nuanced matter. But the line I drew was neither arbitrary nor nuanced. There aren't gradations. Edge cases will sometimes return false positives, while legitimate results will occasionally be excluded.

This problem impacts much more than Dutch porn—think of the difference between milk chocolate and chocolate milk, for example. In fact, any word with multiple meanings, some misspellings, and many unusual combinations of words risk landing on the wrong side of such a hard-line division. The line itself is incredibly useful, but a human touch is needed to bring machine learning's stark decisions into context.

NUANCE

In the early days of Google AdWords, clever marketers who identified a likely misspelling of a keyword associated with their product could skim prospective customers by paying a penny apiece for the typo instead of the correct spelling's much higher price.

Google later addressed this quirk with the broad match keywords described above, using its machine learning program to determine what the most common typos were likely to be. Let me give an example using my company's name.

Far fewer people than my co-founders, Manas and Geetanjali, and I had hoped can correctly spell Optmyzr—a made-up word that was closest to "optimizer" and still available as a domain name. Before broad match keywords, I would have needed to include Optimyzr, Optmizr, Optimizr, and Optimizer, among a dozen other guesses at how people might type our company name wrong, in my keywords. Even today, I'm stunned by how inventively people can misspell OPTMYZR. Yes, O-P-T-M-Y-Z-R, there's no E...remember that please!

To my relief, I don't have this worry anymore, at least when it comes to my company's being found when someone goes to the search bar. Google has invested a great deal in ML programs that can figure out these correlations to my benefit. Why would I build my own system to try to do the same thing? Google can do far more, far better than you or I can, in large part because they get far more data than any of us ever could get from our own website data. (More than two trillion searches are done on Google annually!)

But Google's not done helping. It now applies—no opting out—what's known as "close variants" to each keyword match type: exact match, phrase match, and broad match. Close variants layer on top of all these match types and allow for minor variations to be treated as if they were essentially one of your keywords. Such variations include plurals (tool, tools), typos (tool, toool), stemmings (tool, tooling), and function words (tools, "with tools"). The following table shows all the ways in which Google is allowed to change keywords based on close variant rules:

CLOSE VARIANT MATCHING RULES	KEYWORD	MATCHED QUERY
Misspelling	Optmyzr	Optmyzer
Plural/Singular	Keyword tool	Keyword tools
Stemming	Ad management	Ad manager
Abbreviation	Pay per click	PPC
Accents	Résumé	Resume
Word Count (with same meaning)	Conversion tracking	Tracking conversion
Function words	Pricing for Optmyzr	Pricing Optmyzr
Implied words	RSA ads	RSA
Synonym	Query tool	Search terms tool
Paraphrase	PPC tool	What is a good PPC tool I can buy
Same intent	Optimize shopping ads	PLA management tool

But the degree to which close variants can modify an advertiser's keyword now goes even further, exacerbating the relevancy problem. "Exact match" is no longer very strict and can show ads for searches with supposedly the "same meaning," whatever that means.

Here's an example. Optmyzr advertises on the exact match keyword "ppc management tool." But Google, under the "close variants" rules, decides that someone searching for "ppc management" is essentially looking for the same thing because it's close enough to the "same meaning." Only Optmyzr is dissatisfied, because dropping the word "tool" means the user could be searching for a PPC agency or service provider. We aren't an agency, so the click would be wasted money for us.

Since you don't have the option of excluding close variants,

Google AI now determines if a search term is close enough to one of your keywords to warrant showing a result. Granted, in many if not most cases this may be close enough, provided you want good but average performance. It isn't close enough if you want your marketing campaign to stand out.

A FLORIST'S DILEMMA

Bernard, owner of Bernard Associates, a PPC agency, is hired to handle digital advertising for the national florist chain Betty's Blooms. The agency logically included "floral arrangements" in its list of keyword phrases.

Google then identified close variants of those keyword phrases. It was a good try at being helpful, but unanticipated problems ensued. The system figured that both "flower arrangements" and "arranging flowers" were good close variants of "floral arrangements." And who can blame it?

But as apparently related as the two phrases "floral arrangements" and "arranging flowers" are, they yield very different search results. A person looking for flower arrangements probably needs a florist and is willing to pay a premium for a beautiful bouquet and same-day delivery. Someone searching "arranging flowers" is probably looking for a YouTube video on what to do with the flowers they've just picked from their garden.

Given a choice, Bernard would probably choose to show his ad for the close variant "flower arrangements," but not the variant "arranging flowers." But he doesn't get the choice.

Bernard, like every other advertiser, has to use close variants by default. It's not something advertisers have the option to turn off in Google Ads. If they haven't joined the 70-plus percent of Google advertisers using Smart Bidding, his client will have to pay the same for the less commercial query as for the more appropriate one.

However, if Bernard's agency is also using automated bid management, Google will probably notice—eventually—that few of the users who saw Bernard's ad after having searched on "arranging flowers" went on to make a purchase. It will then lower the bid on that "close variant," but not as quickly as the client might have liked. This is another truth of PPC: we inevitably have to spend some money on getting clicks so that Google's ML can start to work its magic. It's a tax everyone who wants to play has to pay.

If Bernard's agency isn't using automated bid management, his client may notice that "arranging flowers" is considered a close variant of "floral arrangement" and conclude Google Ads doesn't work. Bernard can address the issue, but only if he knows why the system considers "arranging flowers" a close variant in the first place.

What happens is that Google's machine learning assigns a score to a prediction such as "arranging flowers." It doesn't make decisions based on those scores. A Google employee does. A person draws the line that determines what ads to return based on the machine-generated score. That was one of my jobs in the Dutch porn project.

In this case, the algorithm might have determined that "arranging flowers" had an 89.7 percent overlap with the keyword "floral arrangements." In contrast, the search phrase "what is the most common color of roses?" has only a 3 percent correlation.

Say the person at Google sets the threshold at 85 percent. Any search with that or a greater degree of correlation will return the florist's ad. Any below it will not. A person searching for "arranging flowers" will see the Betty's Blooms ad, while those asking the question about the most common color of roses won't.

Advertisers get frustrated when they see their ads served in response to queries not in the keyword list. "Close variants" are great in many instances, but they lack the nuance often required.

Worse still, Google will occasionally change the thresholds governing how the ad auction functions without notifying the advertiser. If the threshold drops from 85 to 80 percent, Bernard will suddenly and inexplicably start to see his client's ad showing up in response to queries he's never seen before. And due to the ever-decreasing access to search terms data, chances are Bernard sees his results decline for a while without being able to pinpoint what negative keywords to add to counteract this.

What's needed is human-plus-machine intervention. Automation layering can solve otherwise intractable problems by identifying close variants that really aren't. We'll return to Bernard's agency and his client in the following chapters.

CREATIVITY
Creativity, like nuance and context, is difficult for machines,

no matter how "intelligent." Google has a long tradition of struggling with the creative components of advertising. The system has the expertise to target specific audiences. But it has no idea what to say to get those audiences to convert.

In *Digital Marketing in an AI World*, I discussed Google's first attempt at what they called Ad Libs. Google provided advertisers a template like that found in the children's game Mad Libs, which they filled in. With predictably abysmal results. The ads looked like what they were—generic, hack-and-paste jobs that looked alike and were easy to ignore.

Responsive Search Ads (RSA), Google's most recent attempt to solve the ad-creation problem, is a huge step up from Ad Libs. It requires advertisers to provide their own lists of value propositions, calls to action, benefits, headlines, descriptions, and the URLs to the pages in their website where traffic should be directed.

Although those who start using RSAs overwhelmingly tend to keep using them, they have their Ad Libs–style limitations. There is widespread skepticism among PPC experts that RSAs are really on a par with ads written and assembled the old-fashioned, human-powered way. But don't count on RSAs becoming less ubiquitous. As covered in my third truth, controls will decrease, so we had better learn how to work with RSAs instead of competing against them.

The ads Google assembles on the fly, despite being highly targeted, don't always perform well for advertisers. Creativity is the missing element advertisers themselves need to supply. Google may help assemble elements, but the quality of those elements is up to you. Think of the world's best-known slogans: Just Do It. Got Milk? A Diamond Is Forever. Think Different. Creative marketing geniuses came up with these, not computers.

Let's look more deeply at the essential human roles in digital advertising.

CHAPTER 4

•

•

•

•

THE HUMAN FACTOR

In *Digital Marketing in an AI World*, I argued that artificial intelligence plus human intelligence was superior to either alone:

HUMANS + MACHINES > MACHINES ALONE

I also introduced and defined the three roles PPC marketers can and must continue to play in the system, calling them teacher, doctor, and pilot.

Teachers train the system, both initially and later as needed to get optimum results. Doctors diagnose problems and hold clients' hands while these are resolved. Pilots monitor performance and take control from the machine when necessary.

In the three years since that book was published, Google's machine learning has continued to advance at a mind-blowing pace. Are the roles of teacher, doctor, and pilot still needed? They are, given the machine's limitations in dealing with context, nuance, and creativity, among other issues.

But the digital marketer's roles today are more complex and individualized than ever before, and the three roles I previously identified have changed accordingly. There's also now a fourth role that only humans can play in the overall system: strategist.

Let's take a look at each.

THE TEACHER

Digital Marketing in an AI World discussed how PPC marketers, in their teacher role, can train or "educate" AI systems, and even, if they have the programming skills, build them. Three years later, PPC teachers still play a critical role in training the automated system so that it provides the best results.

However, it's even truer today that, when all is said and done, you can't compete with Google in creating PPC AI systems. Google Ads AI is so complex and intricate that building a comparable system is beyond the scope of all but the largest advertisers.

What's large? My company, Optmyzr, was recently fired by a client who was big enough that they wanted to build their own solutions to PPC problems. They spent over $500 million annually on performance marketing at the time. We have many clients spending in the $100,000 to several million dollars per year range, and many of those continue to rely on others to build their PPC AI.

Even if you were able to do so, the ROI would not justify the time expended. Teachers can make far better use of their time educating the system about the issues unique to their own accounts. Remember automation layering. Your real power isn't in building a competitor to Google's AI, but rather it is in finding ways to scalably teach it what makes your business unique.

In the earlier mortgage bank example, Betty played the teacher role. She noticed problems developing after deployment of an AI system focused on getting prospective customers to fill out her bank's lead-gen form. She then built a regression model to show how variables—the various factors important to the bank's business—relate to the likelihood of a lead turning into a customer.

Betty discovered which form fills were most highly correlated with her bank's desired outcome: closing mortgages. The quality of the responses to the lead-gen form was far more important than their quantity.

Betty fed that qualitative information back into the system through automation layering, teaching the AI what to weight preferentially. After several iterations, she had taught the system to optimize results.

Betty's ingenuity and creativity played the critical role in this process. The statistical methods she used are readily accessible, and her team was able to create an automation layer that complemented Google's complex system.

THE DOCTOR

The doctor's job is to diagnose the patient's problem and then prescribe the medications or perform the procedures needed to effect a cure. PPC marketers, in the doctor role, troubleshoot and fix problems. They also do something AI systems are terrible at: explaining why there's a problem and otherwise holding the client's hand as the issue is worked through and resolved.

As digital marketing ML complexifies, the system becomes even more of a black box, making the doctor's role more critical than before. A doctor's functions are two-fold. In simpler cases, the PPC marketer becomes Marcus Welby, MD, the avuncular family physician, reassuring the client that everything is going to be alright, while working diligently to make it so.

In more complex cases, the marketer turns into Dr. House, forensic pathologist, a Sherlock Holmes–type figure whose analytical powers get to the bottom of the mystery. The doctor goes through the clues—the system's many variables and options—to diagnose where the problem has arisen.

Google Ads ML is constantly changing and evolving. As new factors are added and old ones superseded, unforeseen interactions and consequences will inevitably arise. The doctor's job is to locate and resolve any harmful interactions that emerge.

Determining what the system has prioritized and how it changes in response to new circumstances requires a sophisticated human intelligence capable of understanding context and nuance. The more accurate and holistic an advertiser's mental model of what makes the business work, the better position you're in to optimize and leverage Google's power to put your business or client ahead of the competition.

THE PILOT

As with the doctor, there are two pilot roles: commercial pilot and fighter pilot. The commercial pilot's role is to monitor the system in real time. In complex maneuvers like taking off and landing, the commercial pilot takes manual control of the plane. Likewise, they wrest control when an issue develops or in an emergency.

Say your client's website goes down. In this PPC emergency, it's critical to lower your bids temporarily, so as to decrease wasted spend. Otherwise, you will keep high bids for clicks that lead nowhere. But a good commercial pilot will also notice optimization opportunities that aren't emergencies, like when ad placement never rises to the first page of search results, and intervene.

Commercial pilots need to monitor the system's dials and gauges to know when it's necessary to intervene. They must also be able to distinguish between an anomaly and a real emergency.

The fighter-pilot role is more proactive. Fighter pilots look at the competitive landscape in real time and decide when and how to exploit competitors' mistakes. To extend the previous examples, fighter pilots may front-load budgets when they notice that a competitor's website has gone down. If they notice that the competitor's ads don't appear on the first results page, they'll act quickly to exploit that advantage and get as many new customers at a lower than typical cost during a lull in the competitive environment.

What makes this role more challenging is that Google doesn't provide a dashboard overview of everything relevant that's going on. Pilots need a cockpit, which can and should be created using third-party tools, a process we'll explore below.

THE STRATEGIST

In *Digital Marketing in an AI World*, I argued that the roles many digital marketers then played were tactical, focusing on button-pushing. Now, thanks to rapidly evolving ML, we have been freed up to focus on more critical strategic tasks.

When I say "button-pusher," I mean that marketers were required to do the same tasks over and over again. Early PPC AI tools were incredibly labor-intensive to operate. Optimizing accounts involved such repetitive tasks as determining which queries called up which ads, adjusting associated keywords and bids, and monitoring results. Ken Chang, who runs digital marketing at Minnesota's Star Tribune Media went on the record during a PPC Town Hall episode with me to say that a day in the life of PPC could be really, really boring!

If you were an analyst, your role wasn't much more inspiring— poring over spreadsheets, choosing keywords, and setting bids. The work was almost entirely about qualifying *who* saw an ad. Little thought was given to *what* they saw.

The emphasis on button-pushing was actually a necessary phase in AI development. In the early days, as marketers became *digital* marketers, the focus on tactics was critical. When keywords were as broad as "hotel" and advertisers had to craft one message to deliver to thousands of undifferentiated potential customers, "Huge selection at bargain prices" was about the most generically useful ad an advertiser could write.

I can't tell you how many times I saw accounts where the advertiser had labored for weeks over keywords and bids, only to write haphazard and generic ads. This seemed in many cases a sort of necessary evil if they wanted their keywords to start running.

In Optmyzr, we have an audit tool that identifies instances when the same ad text is used too often. Again, I see huge accounts, managed by teams of smart PPC professionals, where 80 percent of the headlines in different ad groups all say the exact same thing, even though each ad group clearly has unique keywords.

With Google now using thousands of additional data points to differentiate among *who* is searching for "hotel," and with new audience-targeting options that go beyond keywords, marketers can and should return to their advertising roots and put more time into *what* they say. It's the point in the entire PPC process where they're able to communicate with their audience directly, human-to-human. The strategist supplies the context, nuance, and creativity the system lacks.

As machine learning allows for progressively more targeted audiences, marketers will increasingly be able to talk directly to qualified groups of people with similar demographics and psychographics.

A boutique, urban hotelier and budget motel owner are increasingly unlikely to get much overlap in who sees their ads. Google also has enough information about the characteristics of different groups to know what message is most likely to resonate with each.

A business traveler, for example, might see the hotel ads featuring a flexible cancellation policy and high-speed internet. A cost-conscious family will get ads focused on low prices and a free breakfast buffet.

Button-pushing and data analysis is tedious and time-consuming. In the early days of digital marketing, advertisers were so swamped with detail work that they rarely had the opportunity to be strategic or develop the kind of creative solutions that drive campaigns to the next level.

Creativity often requires blocks of uninterrupted thinking time, which are all but impossible when your day is taken up with multiple manual adjustments to myriad automations. In the more evolved AI landscape, the digital marketer again has time to be creative and come up with new, innovative strategies to unlevel the playing field.

STRATEGIC CREATIVITY

Ninja PPC marketer Martin Röttgerding cites an example of this kind of creativity by his German agency, Bloofusion. Its client, a high-end shoe company, began showing different text ads in response to searches for certain styles based on what was available within a given radius of where the customer lived. The shoe company combined several different automations in real time, determining the customer's location, how far the closest store was, and what it had in stock.

If Hans, for example, searched for a style in a size not in stock within ten miles, the ad directed him to the web page of the company's online store. But if there was an available pair nearby, the ad offered more options. Hans could still place his order online, or he could come into a nearby brick-and-mortar store and try on a pair.

It's obviously important to get this right if you want your brand to create a magical moment for their customer. If the stock-tracking function fails, and Hans drives ten miles to find his local store is sold out of the style or size he wants, he could get a bad taste in his mouth that lingers for years. If things go right, however, he buys a pair of shoes and becomes a customer for life.

Indeed, the potential upside is enormous. Many people are much more willing to invest in an expensive brand of shoes after having tried them on than if they had only seen a photo online.

Some of the Google Ads system's newest offerings require more creativity from the advertiser than used to be the case. For example, as Google is allowing more and more nontext elements onto their search results pages, they've introduced shoppable image ads in which the advertiser submits an image that includes several of their products, each of which is clickable.

An office supply store might show a photo of a workstation featuring a high-end ergonomic chair behind a stylish desk on which the latest-model monitor is tastefully lit by a beautiful lamp. Users doing generic searches like "modern office furniture" are served the showcase shopping ad rather than ads for a specific product. The customer can then click on the lamp, the chair, or the desk and be taken directly to that item's page on the store's site.

This is a fantastic new advertising option. But it requires the office-supply store's digital marketers to go beyond their familiar role of writing ad text.

How should they structure a shoppable image campaign? Which products should they prioritize? What products should be shown together? How is an appealing photographic image to be created?

Even a simpler question like what images to add to an item in a product feed in Google Merchant Center can have a big impact on how many impressions of your shopping ad turn into sales. All of these are strategic and creative tasks that people are good at and AI systems are not.

As strategists, digital marketers reengage with the creative work of advertising, planning campaigns, crafting messages, and developing innovative applications of Google's automations. But with all the buttons and levers Google AI requires us to manage, how are we to free up our time to be strategic?

That's the job of automation layering. Let's take a closer look.

·
·
·
·

CHAPTER 5

WHY AUTOMATION LAYERING?

As Google Ads and its automations have grown increasingly complex, PPC managers have had to develop a new mindset. To meet their company's and clients' unique needs, they've needed to learn to manipulate Google automations without many of the usual controls.

Machine learning automation promises to make PPC professionals' lives easier. This should free them up to be more strategic. But advertisers still have to monitor performance and diagnose problems. I've encountered several advertisers who spend most of their days changing settings for automated tools and pausing or unpausing scripts, which shows that automation can be as big a time drain as doing optimizations entirely by hand.

The average advertiser sees a binary choice: continue button-pushing to manage ads manually or allow Google to take over entirely. A set-it-and-forget-it approach to automation delivers merely average—that is, subpar—results. But foregoing automation gives a leg up to competitors who employ it. So, PPC professionals now push new buttons, and remain chained to their laptops.

The time has come for a new mindshift—the biggest in PPC history.

That's because there's another option: automation layering—inserting simple programs, such as scripts and macros, into the system, enabling you to exert greater control over Google. With this option, combined with carefully cultivated "power user" control over existing system capabilities, you can realize the full promise of PPC in an AI world.

Why isn't Google's system capable of already getting us where we want to go? The short answer is because Google Ads is using an engineering mindset to rebuild an airplane that's already in the air.

AdWords was created when machine learning was in its infancy. At that point, Google could only allow customers to come up with the right keywords, formulate an ad, and do the math to set a profitable bid. Although simple compared to today's AI, AdWords was already a complex system, much like a plane.

Once that plane took off, it never landed. As machine learning and other technology improved, the system was rebuilt several times without ever being taken offline, so that customers experienced no interruption in ad placement and delivery.

And while the system was never taken offline, it did very nearly crash. I remember emergency meetings in Building 42, long the home base of the Ads product team. We had a big issue. Advertisers were dumping entire dictionaries worth of words into their keyword lists. The number of keywords was quickly spiraling out of control. Since every single one had to be considered for every single ad auction, the Ads system was on the verge of collapsing under its own weight.

That's when we decided to introduce a new keyword state, called "low search volume." Any keyword with not enough monthly searches would get this status and become inactive. As the AdWords Evangelist, I can tell you that was a fun one to explain to irate advertisers who felt entitled to load any keyword they damn well pleased into the system.

But back to the airplane that's already taken off. To avoid a crash, rebuilding a plane midflight must be done one part at a time. This is tough, but Google found the process acceptable, because as an organization it always leads with an engineering mindset.

THE ENGINEERING MINDSET

Engineers are trained to break complex problems down into their components and address each in turn. You solve the smaller problems and then string your solutions together to solve the larger, original issue.

Google is an engineering company, while marketing is a very human field. Companies often take on their founders' persona and that's certainly the case with Google. Its founders, Larry Page and Sergey Brin, are brilliant Stanford-educated engineers interested in creating the best but not necessarily the most beautiful search engine. Users love both its simplicity and results.

Because engineers designed, modified, and expanded on Google's advertising framework, its many powerful tools were created with an engineer's mindset. Once we understand how engineers think and see the ways they draw conclusions about what the "typical" or average advertiser needs, we'll see how this can sometimes lead to problems.

Let's say Google's mission was not to "organize the world's information and make it universally accessible and useful," but to build a house with advanced new amenities like fully automated laundry. Engineers tasked with creating this system would first break it down into its components. One team built a conveyer system to transport laundry from the hamper in each walk-in closet to the washing machine in the laundry room, and another group set out to create a better washing machine.

You move into your new home, delighted that your laundry will be washed by a best-of-breed system. Your delight is squashed after your first load of laundry is done: your whites have come out a pale pinkish hue. Google's "improvements" seem to be a step backward.

And you don't know how to solve the problem, since the new laundry system has none of the dials and settings you're used to. Google has hidden all those confusing buttons and knobs with the goal of streamlining the process and making things "easier" for you.

Actually, Google's preset settings will do a great job of washing your clothes, as long as they're all whites and all cotton. This means you've got to help the system along. You need to sort your clothes manually, separating whites from coloreds, for example. But if you've got a big family, or are running a commercial laundry service, you could easily spend a lot of time sorting laundry in what's supposed to be a fully automated system.

You don't need to reinvent the washer and dryer. They work just fine. You need to add a laundry-sorting automation to the system—perhaps a simple robot that runs on an algorithm that instantiates your sorting logic: if white, put in one pile; if colored, put in another.

Of course, it's not so easy to build even a simple robot. That's beyond most of our capabilities. (If it's not, please forward me your résumé.) Fortunately, in Google Ads, we don't need a robot to sort things. Just a bit of spreadsheet magic will achieve a lot.

Here's how this works in Google Ads. When you create a new campaign, Google may default to automated bidding with the goal of "maximizing conversions." But most companies would rather optimize for profits than conversions. If profits matter more than number of sales, you'll likely need to have multiple campaigns, each with a different target ROAS (tROAS), into which all your products will be sorted.

If you have products with a 50 percent margin, you need to have a tROAS of 200 percent to break even. For products with a 33 percent margin, your tROAS is 300 percent. Your products need to be sorted into two different piles representing two different campaigns.

CALCULATING TARGET ROAS

The formula for using margin percentages to calculate break-even tROAS is:

100/margin = Break-even ROAS

For example:

- For products with a 50 percent margin: 100/0.5 = 200. You need a break-even ROAS of 200 percent. In other words, $1 in ad costs should return $2 in sales and with a 50 percent margin, that $2 in sales represents $1 in profit, the same as the ad costs.
- For products with a 33 percent margin: 100/0.33 300. You need a break-even ROAS of 300 percent. So, $1 in ad costs should return $3 in sales and with a 33 percent margin. That $3 in sales represents $1 in profit, again the same as the ad costs, so you break even.

The takeaway is that Google Ads doesn't sort your laundry. Only you can bring together the relevant business data, determine your profit margins, separate your products accordingly, and group them by the ROAS they need to break even. That done, you can confidently put your ads in the system and tell Google what the tROAS is for each of the categories.

Google has built a complex washer based on data from millions of users. You don't need to do your laundry by hand. You simply need to find a way to take back some of the controls you need to make the washer do its job right. You let Google do the real-time, automated bid management, but you achieve far better results by telling the automated system more about how to do the right job for your business.

Again, if you have a laundry service, or even a large family, getting the most out of the Google washing machine would involve far too much hand-sorting. Likewise, if you have a large product catalog, you can't go in every day, figure out profit margins for every new product, and determine how to group them into campaigns with the right targets. Your time is much better spent on strategy.

Marketers need their own automations based on their company's or client's business logic and business rules. They need automations that can adjust and adapt Google's automations. As mentioned earlier, marketers need an automated laundry-sorting robot—or automated spreadsheet—layered between them and Google's automated bidding. Its job is to check for new products, sort them by profit margin, and put the 33 and 50 percent-margin products in the 200 and 300 percent tROAS campaigns.

That is what automation layering can do. As you can see, it doesn't have to be overly complicated to be effective.

Let's return to our earlier examples to see how automation layering can solve some persistent Google Ads problems.

SMART BIDDING: BETTY'S MORTGAGES

One of Google's most advanced automations, Smart Bidding still suffers the consequences of the piecemeal, "engineering mindset" approach described above. To add to the confusion, as of this writing, there were six forms of Google Ads automated bidding, with two additional subtypes, all with significant differences between them.

Some forms of automated bidding periodically set and adjust bids for keywords. Smart Bidding sets bids for every individual auction in real time, which means that it is more precise than other forms of automated bidding. It also takes into account factors such as time of day, the user's location, and which device they're using.

But there are many more factors and even more possible combinations of those factors. According to Google, Smart Bidding considers over 500,000 factors when serving ads on search results and over 70 million factors when serving ads on the Display Network.

Smart Bidding is undoubtedly a much better approach than manual bidding, because it sets bids based on every factor that Google monitors for impact on conversion rates. But advertisers who use Smart Bidding can't set it and forget it, at least if they want to unlevel the playing field.

Bid automation calculates the CPC needed at the ad auction from the tCPA or tROAS, combined with expected conversion rates. The math is simple, but the number of factors Google considers makes the process complex.

Even though bids seem like the factor that most directly impacts the bottom line, there are other important considerations at play when it comes to driving profits. In our mortgage bank example, Betty was absolutely correct to implement Smart Bidding, even though the subsequent increase in conversions didn't translate immediately into more mortgages closed.

Betty's solution was to fix not bids but conversion data. Her team created a relatively sophisticated regression model that scored any leads brought in according to the bank's particular criteria. She then fed that data back into Google, teaching the system to adjust its bids to target what actually mattered to the bank.

Replacing manual bid management with the equally arduous chore of manually reviewing lead quality wouldn't have been much of an improvement. Instead, Betty implemented a nightly regression analysis and used the results to adjust conversion data that was already in Google's system. Layered on top of Smart Bidding, Betty's automation helped Google adjust its bids more accurately, giving the bank an advantage over its competitors, who were either still struggling to manage their bids manually or operating at the mercy of a less-informed automated bid-management system.

SMART SHOPPING CAMPAIGNS: ALONZO'S AUTO PARTS

There are a number of fully automated Smart Campaign types, including Smart Shopping. These ask little input from advertisers and provide correspondingly little control. But even a Smart Shopping campaign can benefit from a strategy devised to unlevel the field.

When we last saw Alonzo, he was relatively satisfied with how Smart Shopping campaigns were working for his auto parts store. Except on freezing mornings, which happen a lot in Michigan. Happily, there was still room for him to take back some control from Google and optimize.

For example, Alonzo could set up a separate campaign for "car batteries." He would then have the option of adjusting just that one set of products according to the weather.

For instance, Alonzo could insert an automation layer, built relatively simply with a Google Ads script that checks the weather forecast, into the system. It could use a public weather API and set a lower tROAS on the first days of a freeze. The lower tROAS indicates to Google that Alonzo is willing to have a lower return on his ad spend. But Alonzo is smart and knows Google isn't paying attention to how the weather impacts his sales. His increased conversion rate on those cold days will more than offset his temporarily higher bids. At the end of the day, he makes more profit, which is what matters to him.

KEYWORD SEARCHES: OPTMYZR

For misspellings of my company's name and keyword variations, I'm happy to let Google calculate the whole universe of possible searches that might be relevant. But I want to be able to make adjustments. I want to differentiate between a person who is clearly searching for my company but has misspelled its name from the person who's searching for a good or service for which Optmyzr might offer only a marginally good fit.

With an automation layer, I can show the first group an ad that answers their questions about my company directly. Remember the key value proposition of Google Ads is that it connects users to companies at the moment of relevance. What better way to indicate relevance than to let the ad answer the user's question? "Looking for better budget controls? Sign up for a trial and try our PPC budget tools today!" This ad is both direct and helpful.

To the second group, brought in with a wider net like that cast by close variants, I can show ads that will help nurture trust by showing some of our best-case studies and industry recognition. "Looking for PPC management services? We don't do the work for you, but our award-winning tools are easy and affordable. Why not give them a try? Perhaps you don't really need services after all."

Because Optmyzr helps advertisers manage keywords, our ads might be triggered when someone searches on "Google Ads keyword tool." If Google decides that's a close variant or a broad match with one of my keywords, it will show my branded ad, which actually says nothing about keyword management and is therefore irrelevant.

To find these low-performing search variations, I could look at the metrics for each specific query manually and see if it has a low click-through rate relative to the other keywords in the same ad group. Alternately, I could use an automation layer to monitor every query that triggers my ad and to identify those with poor click-through rates. The automation layer would then move underperformers to their own ad group and label them for me. Now all I need to do is check those automatically created groups and take the final, creative step myself—writing ad text that addresses the actual intent of the search.

The machine does what it does well—sorting and labeling; I do what machines do poorly—marketing.

AUTOMATION LAYERING BY ROLE

HUMANS + MACHINES > MACHINES ALONE

Since I posited that equation in my previous book, Google's machine learning has continued to improve. The roles of humans in that equation ought to change as well. We will continue playing the roles of teacher, doctor, and pilot. But those roles have to evolve to enable account managers to become more strategic than tactical.

Previously, if an automation wasn't working well, teachers asked: what more training could I have given these task-based automations to make them perform better?

Doctors asked: What ails the patient? What solutions can we put in place to effect a cure?

Pilots asked: How do we know what is and isn't working? How do we take control when something's wrong?

How have those roles evolved in the rapidly changing PPC landscape? In many cases, this involves automation layering.

THE TEACHER

Let's return to our example of Joe's Photo Shop. Imagine that Joe has brought his PPC-savvy son Joe Jr. into the business. Junior creates multiple campaigns with different targets. He is happy to use automated bidding but sets out to teach the system the specifics of his dad's business.

Joe Jr. teaches Google ML about the camera shop's promotional calendar. Especially which weekends his dad will be offering big discounts and how to change their automated bid strategies accordingly.

Google's Seasonality Adjustments feature is designed specifically to interact with its automated bidding and adjust for changes that occur over a short time period. If Joe's sales volume or conversion rate changes, Google's automated system adjusts its predictions accordingly. On the other hand, if Joe expects an upcoming sale will have a short-term impact on conversion rates and sales volume, Joe Jr. can teach the AI to expect this change.

Each time his dad has a sale coming up, Joe Jr. manually logs into Google and teaches it this lesson. But Joe Jr. could really unlevel the playing field by creating an automation layer that does this for him.

Joe already has all the promotions he's planned on a spreadsheet. The automation layer refers to the spreadsheet, and when it notices an upcoming seasonal promotion, it goes into Google and sets the seasonality bid adjustments.

When Bernard's PPC agency went in and made "arranging flowers" a negative search term for Betty's Blooms, it was acting in the teacher role.

In AdWords' early days, it was possible to specify the exact keywords that triggered an ad. Over time, Google broadened how it defines keywords, and borders have become fuzzy. Google has effectively eliminated exact match keywords by introducing "close variants." Now, Google shows Bernard's ad anytime it believes the user is searching for something with the "same meaning" as one of his keywords. Xavier can no longer tell Google to only show Bernard's ad if the user searches for a specific string of words.

"Close variants" is on by default. There is no "opt in/opt out" toggle switch. That's why Bernard's agency, again putting on its teacher hat, monitors automatic broadening of keywords and the resulting search terms more closely than other parts of the system.

To automate this surveillance, Bernard and his team could create an automation layer that watched for certain words or phrases in queries. If the word "arranging" or the phrase "how to arrange" showed up in a new ad group, the automation layer would automatically add it as a negative keyword. They could of course also add this to a negative list shared by all campaigns in the account, which would prohibit this search phrase from showing any of his client's ads.

Bernard and his team could go a step further and create an automation layer that benefits all their florist clients. When they discover a less-than-ideal close variant like "how to arrange flowers" in one ad group, they could use a script to add a negative keyword to all florist accounts, who would all profit from having hired an agency with deep expertise in the florist industry.

Bernard could also employ a metrics-driven automation layer focusing on conversion rates rather than click-through rates. His client doesn't care what prompts someone to click on his ad. He cares about what gets *people who will buy flowers from his client* to click.

Google now has an "optimization score" for every campaign and ad in Google Ads. Visiting the "Recommendations" tab generates a list of suggestions—what Google's AI thinks the advertiser could do to make the campaign or ad group perform better. The recommendations are based on the notion of "headroom" or how much opportunity exists in different parts of the account to gain additional sales and conversions. These recommendations often include a list of new keywords to consider, based on searches Google has determined may be relevant to what is being advertised.

As an example, Google suggested Optmyzr consider "What are keyword match types?" as a keyword phrase. Google knows Optmyzr sells PPC management software, so questions about keyword match types are certainly relevant to my business. The phrase is absolutely apropos, but not a great choice for a keyword phrase if my actual advertising goal is to connect to new customers and close sales.

(By the way, while Google may also know I'm writing a book, I'd like to think it doesn't know I'd be needing exactly such an example to illustrate this point.)

At Optmyzr, we use Google's recommendations as a baseline but run some additional analysis on top of the suggestions to make sure they truly meet our business's goals and not just Google's. Since the Google recommendations can be retrieved programmatically, it is possible for any advertiser to create this type of automation layer.

For some time, advertisers didn't know how quickly automated bidding could adjust for unexpected changes in patterns. Predictable, season-based fluctuations, such as Black Friday, could easily be adjusted for. But what about unforeseen changes?

When the COVID-19 pandemic happened, we indeed found that automated bidding generally works well when a pattern changes abruptly. Most advertisers who used automated bidding saw their bids react quickly and appropriately. The travel vertical saw a steep drop-off in bookings, and Google quickly adjusted those bids downwards. Online retailers selling the tools needed to work from home, on the other hand, saw spikes in conversion rates, and bids kept pace in delivering a consistently positive ROAS.

The advertisers who performed best, however, were the ones with automation layers in place. Some used tools like Opt-myzr's Campaign Automator to keep search ads and keywords dynamically in sync with inventory. When supply chain issues interrupted sales of webcams, for instance, advertisers with their own automated controls quickly saw their ads go offline for products they couldn't have sold even if they wanted to.

Other advertisers had teammates who abruptly became quarantined somewhere without access to their work computers. The ones with automation layers in place continued to drive great results, because these smart automations were already used to manage tedious day-to-day operations more efficiently. A single PPC manager could tweak targets or strategy and trust that the controls they'd created to manage Google's systems would continue to drive the results they expected.

THE DOCTOR

Automation layering has somewhat less impact on the doctor role than the teacher or pilot, as the doctor's role is essentially human. You can't automate bedside manner.

Automation layering can, however, make the doctor's task of generating reports much easier. Even so, the automation supplements rather than replaces the doctor's job. The doctor still needs to walk clients and company executives through the reports, explaining these in easy-to-comprehend language free from marketing jargon. Of course, Google could automatically issue reports directly to clients, but without the human touch, that could create more confusion than illumination.

The doctor can still deploy automation layers to the reporting function, perhaps by using an off-the-shelf tool for generating summaries. But the tool may not collect a key piece of data the agency would like to share with the client every month: for example, how many hours are being billed.

Rather than revert to manual report generation, the agency ports the billing data into the reporting tool through a Google spreadsheet or a service that connects several of today's common SaaS solutions, like Zapier. There are now two layers of automation on top of Google AI: the reporting software and the Google spreadsheet that brings in additional data clients want to see.

Another challenge in reporting is how to show actual advertising costs after regional surcharges or taxes have been added. In countries like France and the UK, Google is passing on a 2 percent regulatory tax to advertisers. Because this fee is billed periodically and not reflected in the cost of every click and its CPC, reports get out of whack. The $10,000 you spent on ads all of a sudden becomes $10,200. Those $100 CPAs become $102 CPAs. It may seem like a small difference, but it throws off how you report and optimize accounts. The solution is to use calculated metrics and derived columns in your reporting and optimization software.

A one-time investment in building these automation layers will pay off in countless hours saved down the road.

THE PILOT

A commercial or fighter pilot is in charge of extremely sophisticated technology. So are PPC pilots. The jet pilot doesn't need to manually adjust navigation, since computers do a much better job of correcting a plane's subtle drifts.

Likewise, even if it were possible, the PPC pilot doesn't want to decide which ad to show to which user and how much to bid in every single search. There are simply too many critical inputs to monitor each manually.

The problem as things stand is that these inputs are located in too many different places. It's like trying to fly a plane with each of the critical dials and gauges kept in its own room rather than assembled in the cockpit. The PPC pilot has to move among them, making necessary adjustments to each while trying to keep an eye on both the horizon and the destination.

A pilot can't simultaneously watch airspeed, altitude, heading, engine performance, and the hundreds of other factors involved in keeping a plane in the air. Nor can the digital marketer interpret how each of the hundreds of signals associated with every search contributes to the likelihood of conversion. As a PPC pilot, you need a cockpit-like interface—a way to monitor how well the automation is managing those tasks for us.

Here's an example. It may not be pretty, but it's functional and uses tools, such as spreadsheets, you already know how to use.

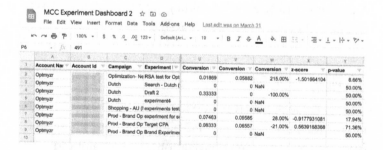

Bernard's agency always tests any new practice using split or A/B experiments to confirm the validity of his theories about what will work best for his clients. Both Google and Microsoft give marketers an automated tool for experimenting using an existing campaign as the control. Called "Drafts and Experiments" in Google, this tool splits ad impressions between whatever the advertiser wants to test—for example, manual bids versus automated bids—and issues a verdict on which performed better.

Since it has multiple clients, the agency frequently runs dozens of experiments at a time. Monitoring them all in his pilot role, Bernard needs a dashboard where he can check on them all without having to go into every account individually. Google's interface doesn't have a view that shows all experiments with all metrics. To get the data he needs, Bernard spends a lot of time clicking around accounts and switching between experiments he wants to analyze.

In this case, being an effective PPC pilot requires an automation layer that pulls together the data from all the experiments the agency is running and puts it on a single spreadsheet or interface. This is a simple and obvious fix that saves Bernard a tremendous amount of time and irritation.

By adding a layer of automation on top of Google's testing framework, Bernard's agency creates a cockpit dashboard that simplifies his job as a pilot. With a more accurate visualization of what's going on, he is in a much better position to make decisions about Betty's Blooms' and his other clients' accounts.

PPC pilots may also want to detect anomalies based on relative values rather than absolutes. It's often very difficult to know at exactly what level of CPA an account truly is in bad shape. So, setting a hard-limit CPA alert can be difficult to do because the pilot may not know what level to choose. But using a Rule Engine, they can build automation layers that look for relative anomalies—for example, campaigns where impressions have dropped at least 10 percent for three weeks in a row.

A word of warning for PPC pilots: a recent *Wall Street Journal* article reported that both airlines and safety experts are worried about pilots' manual flying skills eroding because of the reliance on autopilots. This can reduce hand–eye coordination and confidence in being able to respond correctly to an emergency.

Likewise, PPC professionals need to keep their skills and grasp of the fundamentals polished and up-to-date. Ultimately, even an AI-enabled system doesn't run itself.

PART 1 SUMMARY

ORIENTATION

PPC marketing is a dizzyingly evolving industry. To do your job well, it's essential to keep up.

There are three truths or factors that will keep the industry challenging:

1. Ad platforms will continue to automate.
2. Advertisers will have less access to data going forward.
3. Advertiser control over targeting, bidding, and messaging will keep decreasing.

While Google Ads' artificial intelligence (AI) and machine learning (ML) can produce amazing results, these are also often subpar or just average because they prioritize what's important for Google—click-through rate—over what's important for your or your client's business. This levels what is essentially a highly competitive playing field.

Also, Google AI isn't adept at supplying the context, nuance, and creativity that often separate a successful ad from an unsuccessful one. These only you can furnish.

In my first book, I identified three roles humans must still play in an automated system:

1. Teacher: who trains the system.
2. Doctor: who analyzes problems, knows the pros and cons of different treatments, and holds the client's hand as they are resolved.
3. Pilot: who takes over from the system when issues develop or opportunities arise.

These roles remain just as relevant now, and are joined by a fourth:

4. Strategist: who brings in the creativity, context, and nuance the system otherwise lacks.

As Google Ads complexifies, these roles remain critical, although their focus continues to shift. Now, it's become increasingly important for teachers, doctors, pilots, and strategists to unlevel the playing field through automation layering, which involves inserting or layering relatively compact programs or automations between you and Google AI.

Why? To wrest control back from the system and prioritize your company's or client's business needs over Google Ads'.

Now that you've oriented yourself to today's PPC AI landscape, let's move from the why to the how: the methodology behind unleveling the playing field.

PART 2

METHODOLOGY

CHAPTER 6

•

•

•

•

ACCOUNT STRUCTURE

The average PPC marketer is still using campaign structures developed in response to how Google AdWords operated before automation was fully established. Many of these structures may be sound, but most are outdated, giving the savvy advertiser another arena for unleveling the playing field.

Everyone has a theory about how Google Ads campaigns should be structured. But few have found the optimal balance between the amount of control they want to exert and the ease of simply following Google's advice.

But how you structure your campaigns can give you another way to excel. And the right account structure can also position you to get the most from the tools Google offers and the automation layers that can optimize them.

THE FUNDAMENTALS: AD AND PRODUCT GROUPS

Let's start with some basic definitions. An ad group is one or more ads within a campaign that have the same targeting and goals. Goals could be tROAS for products, tCPA for services, or CPC for advertisers who bid manually. Targeting defines who should see the ads in the ad group. In search campaigns, these targets are keywords. In shopping campaigns, targets are called product groups, which encompass one or more products that have something in common like product category. For example: all products in the category of "walking shoes," "running shoes," or "cleats." Or all sneakers from particular brands like "Adidas sneakers," "Nike sneakers," or "Reebok sneakers."

In shopping campaigns, a product group is also a subset of inventory, all of which share the same bid. There are no associated keywords. Instead, the merchant feed you submit to Google Ads is indexed and used to match products to queries. The shopping campaign product group becomes the equivalent of a keyword in a search campaign ad group.

GRANULARITY AND CONTROL

Many of the most popular structures still in use today are simply what was once necessary to manage an account with the desired level of granularity. If you wanted to make adjustments to small fractions of a given campaign, you needed to create additional ad groups. The more ad groups you had, the more control you had, but the more ad groups you also had to manage. As always, there's a trade-off between control and ease of use.

Google's automations now make many of these account structures unnecessary. For example, advertisers used to create multiple campaigns for the same products so they could show different ads depending on what device the user was searching from. That made sense since people behave differently when they see ads on desktop or mobile devices. In the early days of smartphones, conversion rates were much lower for mobile devices. By having two campaigns, one for mobile and one for desktops, advertisers gave themselves the ability to set different bids by device and ensured they didn't pay the same for a click made on a phone, which was much less likely to lead to a sale. Of course, nowadays most searches and conversions happen on mobile devices, so the script has flipped.

But creating campaigns by device type is no longer required. Google's automated bidding accounts for differences in conversion rates by device type and adjusts bids accordingly, eliminating the need for separate mobile and desktop campaigns.

Today's Smart Shopping campaigns require almost no structure. You can put all your company's products into a single campaign, even if you have a million-item catalog. But you must be willing to trust the automated system to manage it, recognizing that any lever you pull, like budget or target ROAS, will impact every product in exactly the same way.

This doesn't work if you want any control over how portions of a campaign function. In that case, a more granular structure is needed. Let's look at some options.

GRIP

GRIP stands for "GRoup of Individual Products." Each GRIP

is a product group with a single product ID. A GRIP structure allows advertisers to deploy different bids for each product because the bid is set at the product group level.

GRIP Structure Allows for More Precise Bidding

By maintaining groups of individual products (GRIP) structure, you can bid the right amount for every product you sell.

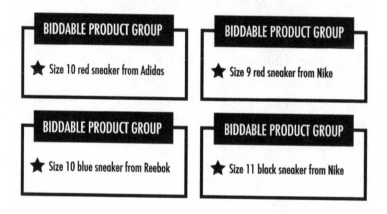

A GRIP structure enables advertisers to make changes to any part of a product catalog without impacting the rest. When every product is a group of one, your control is maximized. With an automation layer managing your groups, this can be done with minimum manual effort. Automation layering makes GRIPs far more manageable, eliminating many of the concerns marketers have with them.

No **GRIP** Structure

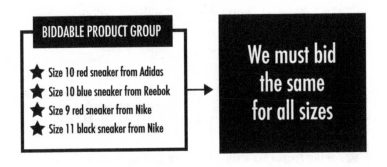

Let's look at the advantages of different implementations of a GRIP account structure.

Shoes Unlimited is a new site in direct competition with Zappos. If it took Google's advice for advertisers using Smart Bidding and ran just a handful of campaigns with a few ad groups each, it might have all Nike shoes in one ad group and all Adidas in another.

This works well when the company wants to run a promotion on Nikes. On the other hand, if marketing wants to see whether blue Nikes sell as well as black ones, it has set itself up for the tough job of manually sorting through all the data. Its campaigns are split by brand, and different colors are mixed randomly among the product groups.

Worse still, if it's discovered blue shoes convert at a lower rate than black ones, meaning that bids should be lowered, the company is out of luck. Its campaign-by-brand structure makes it impossible to lower bids on blue Nikes without also lowering bids on black ones.

If the campaign was restructured into a GRIP that put just one product into each group, marketing would have much more flexibility in determining bids. An automation layer could again quickly find the dozens of "Nike blue shoes" product groups and adjust only those bids appropriately.

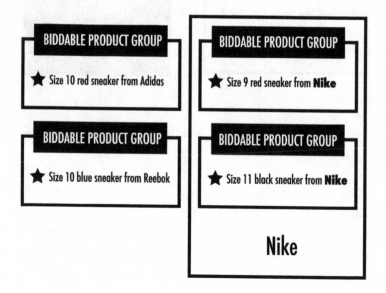

If, as another example, due to changing seasons, all-weather shoes started to convert better than sandals, adjustments to every product meeting "all-weather" criteria could be made without impacting unrelated products. But if, for example, customers have little to no interest in white waterproof shoes, the company could make sure that, when people search for waterproof shoes, ads for white waterproofs are deprioritized by setting a lower bid or even a lower campaign priority.

Similarly, grouping sneakers by sizes will enable you to determine both which size (or sizes) sells best and to raise bids on that size only.

What Size Sells Best

SIZE	CLICKS	COST	CONV VAL/COST
10.5	3102	3922	574%
10	1106	1435	0%
11.2	398	351	0%
11.5	**5911**	**7206**	**1,361%**
11.7	103	940	0%
11	825	1318	838%
12.0	110	590	0%
12.5	2472	3459	289%

BIDDABLE PRODUCT GROUP

⭐ Size **11.5** red sneaker from Adidas

BIDDABLE PRODUCT GROUP

⭐ Size 9 red sneaker from Nike

BIDDABLE PRODUCT GROUP

⭐ Size **11.5** blue sneaker from Reebok

BIDDABLE PRODUCT GROUP

⭐ Size 11 black sneaker from Nike

Size 11.5: Raise bids

Housing multiple products within a single product group is easier to scale manually, but this supposed management efficiency compromises control. A GRIP structure gives marketers the benefits of using Google's automations while still retaining a level of control. While, again, it's all a matter of balancing level of control with ease of use, automation layering can help you take advantage of both sides of this dichotomy.

SPAG

There's also a way for creating a shopping campaign structure where each product has its own ad group, as opposed to product group. This is a SPAG or single-product ad group. A SPAG yields even more control in that it allows adding negative keywords for individual products. Because negative keywords are maintained at the ad group level, placing each product in a separate ad group enables this strategy.

This can be useful, for example, when Google shows a less popular product for a more generic search. As a seller of T-shirts in every color may experience, a search for "T-shirts" sometimes triggers an ad for a neon yellow shirt. But a white or black shirt is probably more likely to be what the user was looking for. Sure, the yellow one is eye-catching but doesn't convert well. The seller of T-shirts can add the negative keyword "-T-shirts" in the SPAG with the neon yellow shirt, thereby telling Google to stop serving an ad for this product on the generic T-shirts query.

This process can be cumbersome when managing thousands of products, but that makes it a prime example of a potential automation layer like the one we have in Optmyzr.

SPAG is Like GRIP
but with More Ad Groups

SKAG

In search campaigns, the equivalent of a SPAG (Single Product Ad Group) is a SKAG, a Single Keyword Ad Group. SKAGs are somewhat (scratch that...they are VERY) controversial, and some marketers don't like to use them at all. But the options here aren't just all or nothing.

Let's return to Bernard's PPC agency. One of his other clients is a national pet food company. They've found that a large, eco-conscious subset of cat lovers would prefer to feed their cat organic food and have created a product to meet this demand.

Bernard's agency creates a SKAG with the keyword "organic cat food." Any customer that searches on that phrase will be delivered an ad for that product with text specifically touting just how organic it is. It might even mention how eco-conscious and progressive the company is, with a couple of well-placed examples. Knowing that a customer who types this phrase and then finds this unique new product is far more likely to convert, bids would be raised.

If this sounds a little like having one shelf for each book in a library, it's because it is. Indeed, it would be quite difficult to find anything in such a system. Shelving books by topic or type, as in the Dewey decimal system, allows for browsing and helps people understand how one category relates to another.

A one-shelf-per-book system only makes sense if humans never go into the library stacks and only order specific books by their titles from a robot that retrieves them. An automation layer can act as just this sort of robot.

Ultimately, this is another trade-off between ease of use and control. Again, all or nothing isn't a helpful perspective. In fact, "skagging" an entire account makes little sense, even with great automation layers. But it does make sense for some of your highest-volume, most important keywords.

In these cases, why wouldn't you want to have that extra control over exactly what your ads say and how much you're bidding, regardless of whether your bid is a maximum CPC, tCPA, or tROAS? You don't need to "skag" every item in your catalog to benefit from becoming a Google Ads power user.

Of course, this isn't the right answer for everyone. One e-commerce advertiser might reasonably stick with a simple structure and run a Smart Shopping campaign with a tROAS. Another one might want more control and have a correspondingly more detailed structure, splitting products among groups based on brand, function, and popularity. Both structures are fine as long as they're consistent and chosen with a clear business purpose in mind.

CAMPAIGN SPLITS

Thanks to Smart Bidding, Google says it's completely fine for advertisers to have a super flat account structure with no granularity: one campaign for everything. This certainly increases ease of use but reduces the control that could well yield better results. There is a middle ground between these approaches, however, that can be deployed at the campaign as well as the ad and product levels.

Many advertisers place themselves at a disadvantage by ignoring or dismissing this more nuanced approach. It makes much more sense to avail yourself of all the available structural possibilities on an as-needed basis.

Google's advice to the contrary, one campaign doesn't necessarily fit all. It often makes sense to group products into different campaigns by seasonality, geography, and profit margin.

For a general merchandise retailer giant like Target, products are even more seasonal than they are for Alonzo and his car batteries. People need car batteries all year, but they only buy plastic eggs and Peeps just before Easter.

For Target, grouping the products it will put on sale together makes good sense. It's fine if all the same rules apply to all Easter decorations. For retailers with several sets of products that are likely to be in high demand at the same time, grouping them together in the same campaign allows them to adjust their bids and budgets together.

Companies with only a few products with regional or geographic variation can use the same strategy for different reasons. If a European home-furnishing firm manufactures high-end patio furniture sold from Sicily to Helsinki, it won't want to run the same ads in both places in February.

Easter may fall on the same day for everyone, but not everyone will want to celebrate it out on the patio. Instead, its agency can create multiple campaigns for the same products for different regional audiences.

These suggestions are summarized in the following chart:

Use Multiple Campaigns to Support Different Business Goals

	CAMPAIGN #1	CAMPAIGN #2	CAMPAIGN #3
PRODUCT CATEGORY	Easter decoration	Patio furniture	Car accessories
SEASONALITY	Popular around Easter	Popular in summer	Popular year-around
TROAS	400% before Easter 100% after Easter	500% until September 1 200% until September 30 75% from October 1	600% year-around

By grouping seasonal items into different campaigns, advertisers can set less aggressive ROAS targets when it's time to liquidate inventory when items are no longer in season.

The third reason for a granular structure is a need to group by budget allocation. For example, Nelson's Nissan dealership might create separate campaigns for the cars he sells and his service department. Because profitability varies significantly among these divisions, Nelson will budget differently for each and set different ROAS targets.

If selling used cars is more profitable than selling new ones—which is counterintuitively actually the case at most dealerships—Nelson might structure his campaign to spend as much as possible on his secondhand inventory and whatever remains on the latest models. Then, if Nissan offers its dealers a limited-time incentive, Nelson can easily reallocate his ad budget to his new car inventory for the duration of the promotion. He might spend more on new cars and keep his ad spend the same for his used cars, or he might reallocate some of those funds.

Every business manages budgets and promotions differently. Savvy advertisers will base their campaign structure on how their business operates and which levers they most need to be able to pull. There is no such thing as a perfect campaign structure, but there is one that's best for your business. Only you have to tailor it yourself.

AD CUSTOMIZERS

Just as there are many good business-driven reasons—like seasonality, geography, and budget allocation—for creating more granular structures, there are two bad reasons for doing so. First off, don't go with more granular structures like GRIP, SKAG, or SPAG thinking you can outmaneuver Google's automations. You can't.

Second, don't go hypergranular when you can get most of the same positive results more simply. If Bernard, for example, wanted to advertise his client's delivery time, he doesn't need to create a new ad for every city in which Betty's Blooms has a store. Rather than creating separate "Buy flowers today—delivery in four hours if you live in New Jersey" and "Buy flowers today—delivery in Manhattan in under two hours" ads, Bernard could run one "Buy flowers today!" ad and use a Google ad customizer to tie the second line to an automatically determined geo identifier.

Not only can the delivery time be automatically inserted in an ad, but now Google even lets advertisers automatically insert the location of the searcher into a responsive search ad (RSA) by simply adding the text {LOCATION(City)} to the ad.

Ad customizers allow marketers to bring highly relevant business data into the ads Google serves. This highlights the competitive advantage of becoming a Google Ads power user.

For example, Joe Jr. at Joe's Photo Shop might want to use a customizer to make a time- rather than location-based template for the firm's ads. They might want to run one ad for the first few days of a promotion and another ("Buy NOW and save") for the last few.

Without a customizer, Bernard and Joe Jr. would need to make separate campaigns for different locales or dates. Using an automation layer like an ad customizer to insert an automatic countdown timer in the ad, they can create a template that uses their unique business data to make their ads more compelling. After all, when users see that a promotion will end in two hours, it's likely they will respond now rather than put off their decision until tomorrow. This is especially true with merchants who have liberal return policies and where the prospective buyer is left with an easy decision: buy it right now with a discount (and return it free if you change your mind) OR buy it later for a higher price.

But there is a downside. A customizer gives you the ease of managing a single campaign. But you lose the ability to compare the performance of the ads' different versions. Only if you write out every single variation of an ad can you get version-specific reports. Using a customizer streamlines things, but performance is visible only for the underlying template, not for each instance or item.

For Carrie, who is in charge of digital advertising for a major recruitment company's online career board, ad customization is a no-brainer. If she creates a customizer that creates ads based on the template "Find X [job type] in Y [city]," then the performance data for that ad will include both the searches for "Find an engineering job in Boise" and those for "Find a paralegal job in Chicago." In other words, the metrics she sees are an average for all cities and job types. That may not be useful to help her optimize things.

It's a judgment call. If Bernard offers under-two-hour delivery in Manhattan, Washington DC, and Boston—Betty's Blooms' most profitable markets—he might do better creating a different campaign for each city. But if he has customized his ad by zip code within those cities, it might not be worth the increased complexity and time drain of creating many different ads to get more insight into how the ad performs neighborhood by neighborhood.

Carrie, on the other hand, might do better to create different customizers for "Find X (job type) in Boise," if she wants to know the ad performance by location, or "Find an engineering job in Y," if she wants to know the same ad's performance by job type. If she wants to see the most granular data, however, she'd have to create ads for every possible combination from "Find an accounting job in Albany" to "Find a zookeeping job in Zurich."

On top of Google's Ad Customizer, Carrie could also use an automation layer, such as Optmyzr's Campaign Automator, to fully write out each ad based on her template and business data, creating thousands of unique and super relevant ad groups in under thirty seconds. This would give her all the advantages of getting more in-depth data on the performance of each variation, without having to create them herself. Because such highly specific ads drive much higher conversion rates, Carrie would unlevel the playing field for her company.

For a more futuristic example, let's imagine a national plumbing chain with fleet-tracking software and GPS in their company vehicles. They could create a "Get a Plumber to Your Door in X Minutes" ad template that would replace the X with a value based on two parameters: the search location and a spreadsheet of where the plumbing company has offices. If the company had fleet-tracking software and GPS in their company vehicles, another automation layer could make the ad even more dynamic by calculating the time estimate based on where individual plumbers are actually located at the time of the search, cross-referenced with its booking system.

If a customer in Cupertino searches for a plumber, the automation layer could "see" that one of the company's plumbers is finishing up a job near Wolfe Road and Old San Francisco Road, with nothing scheduled for the next two hours, and populate the ad template based on this data. The person doing the search would then see an ad saying, "Based on live data, we can get a plumber to your door in 15 minutes."

The customer is likely to book on the spot. The plumbing company fills an empty slot in its schedule, increasing efficiency and possibly saving some drywall!

BE CONSISTENT

Regardless of the structure you settle on, it's critically important to be consistent. Machines are very literal and not as able to adapt for minor variations as humans are. Keep your spelling, capitalization, categories, and groups the same across campaigns.

HUMAN + MACHINE

Robotic vacuum cleaners are a terrific example of how literal-minded machines can be. Their prime directive seems to be "if you can roll over it, suck it up!" This is great for crumbs and dust, not so much for other debris. My Roomba robot-vacuum easily rolls over my kids' socks but can't quite ingest them. The Roomba gets stuck, and the sock gets ruined.

Our pets will occasionally leave a hairball (or worse) on the floor. The Roomba rolls over these deposits and cheerfully spreads the bad news across my whole carpet. As a result, when I want to run my Roomba to clean up crumbs after dinner, I'll move some chairs around to keep it trapped in the dining room. Within that clearly defined environment, it does a fantastic job.

Since, in the PPC world, account structures and naming conventions serve the same environment-delineating function as my wall of chairs, automations can be trusted to stay where they're wanted and do what you like only to the extent that those structures and conventions keep them confined with precision.

To show the havoc inconsistency can wreak, let's return to Nelson's Nissans car dealership. One week, some new inventory was entered as "Nissan Altimas" in a group that had been labeled "Nissan Altima" initially. Nelson had set a monthly $1,000 budget, created individual ad groups for each model, and installed an automation layer that would check every hour for the aggregate spent advertising his Nissans and pause it once it reached $1,000.

The automation layer dutifully monitored bids on Nissan Altima, Nissan Versa, and Nissan Maxima, but it did not count "Nissan Altimas" in the total. As a result, Nelson ended up spending $200 more than he'd budgeted.

GRANULARITY AND SMART BIDDING

Many sophisticated advertisers have chosen to use granular campaign structures to maintain more control. Some advertisers fall in the trap of ceding control they get with granularity (like that GRIPs or SKAGs provide) to satisfy Google's plea to give their machine learning systems more data by removing granularity.

However, a SKAG structure can make more sense for advertisers who use Google's Smart Bidding. Unfortunately, a critical misconception about the number of conversions Smart Bidding needs to be effective has kept many marketers from making the most of it.

For some time, Google Smart Bidding required a minimum of fifty conversions a month. Fewer didn't provide the AI with enough information to ensure Smart Bidding worked well. Google has meanwhile steadily lowered that target as its system has gotten more proficient, but the "fifty conversions minimum" idea lingers in people's minds.

Machine learning models thrive when they have more data, so unsurprisingly, there's general agreement that more conversions equate to better performance, as the system is better able to predict what to bid, lowering CPA and increasing ROAS. This has led to many making the erroneous assumption that by decreasing the granularity of their campaigns, they'll get better results, because conversion data won't be spread too thin across many campaigns, but rather be concentrated in fewer campaigns. The belief is that one campaign with fifty conversions will outperform that same campaign split into ten campaigns with five conversions each. That is a false assumption.

Let's look at Joe's Photo Shop again. Joe Jr. first turned Smart Bidding on with high hopes for his dad's camera sales but was disappointed by the results. Believing that his granular campaign structure might be at fault, he started grouping products together. Soon, rather than one keyword per ad group, he had a hundred and was getting 700 clicks a month on average for each group. He was confident he was helping the system learn more effectively.

Joe Jr. didn't really understand the way Smart Bidding works. As we've seen, with every search, Google factors in an enormous range of data points in addition to search terms: location, time of day, and user demographics. It then compares this entire data set to whatever Joe Jr. has defined as a conversion—his desired outcome whether it's viewing a key page on the website, signing up for a mailing list, or selling a camera.

Google bases its predictions of future conversions on the

relationship between the conversion and the auction leading up to it. Campaign structure plays no part in its predictions. It cares only about how a conversion is defined and what is most likely to lead to one. That means that attribution models, which are discussed in the next chapter, come into play.

Smart Bidding Uses All Conversion Data

CAMPAIGN	BID STRATEGY	CONV.
Branded search	Automated	127
Generic search		74
Remarketing		52
Product line 1	Manual	16
Product line 2		9

Conversion data from manual campaigns impacts automated campaigns.

Even if Joe Jr. weren't using Smart Bidding on every campaign, Google would still be using all the same data to inform the conversion-rate prediction for the campaigns that were using bid automation. Google's conversion-tracking JavaScript code tracks all conversions for an account or a client manager account once it's installed. Google can use that data to "train" or educate the AI and improve the performance for the campaigns for which Joe has turned on Smart Bidding, even though the training data wasn't limited to just the campaigns on Smart Bidding.

Advertisers can then use another unleveling tactic to restate the value of their conversions—which are more and which are less valuable—using a system called "conversion value adjustments" or "offline conversion tracking (OCT)."

While decreasing campaign granularity won't affect Smart Bidding performance, very granular structures do have a downside. Google's competitive-benchmark system, which stacks your ads up for comparison with the competition, can't operate. Competitive benchmarking compares product groups against CPC and CTR (click-through rate) benchmarks, and to protect sensitive data from being seen by competitors, they won't show benchmark data for groups of one product.

Conversely, when there are too many products in a product group, the feedback you get won't be useful. Strive to find a balance between sufficient granularity to get the results you need without getting so much that it becomes meaningless.

The average marketer probably doesn't recognize the need to find this Goldilocks level of granularity, but here again, automation layering can make the most of these subtle differences. A sophisticated automation layer will find a good balance and adjust it on the fly.

For example, you could dynamically vary your account structure from more to less granular based on such factors as the number of clicks you're getting. Several low-click-volume product groups could be combined through a regrouping process.

This makes sense because granularity bestows little advantage for low-volume products. By grouping them together, you'd get competitive benchmark data that could lead to findings such as the low volume being caused by wildly uncompetitive bids. Once that is addressed, and the products pick up new volume, they could be split into more granular SPAGs in order to let you set better bids and add negative keywords.

As feedback fluctuates between too sparse or too plentiful, product-group granularity will increase and decrease to get the best benchmark data.

All this, of course, depends on the accuracy and relevance of any data entered into and received from the system. The methodology behind how you measure input and results is therefore just as critical as account structure. Let's look at which measurement and reporting procedures work in the AI world, and which don't.

CHAPTER 7

.
.
.
.

MEASUREMENT & REPORTING

Google Ads has built-in structural limits, controlling, for example, how many campaigns you can have in an account. However, ever since the introduction of AdWords, the most successful Google advertisers are those who have pushed those limits.

Advertisers who have used measurement feedback at increasingly granular levels, and then acted on the resulting insights by experimenting with new campaign structures, have consistently pushed the field a few extra degrees in their favor.

These more granular structures, discussed in the last chapter, defeat the portfolio effect, in which the averaging of results allows high performers to mask underperformers' poor output. Savvy advertisers have moved away from measuring the performance of the whole—a campaign or ad group—to measuring each of the constituent parts, which is possible only when measurement and reporting are pushed beyond Google's default limits.

Proper measurement allows for a better understanding of cost. A concomitant improved understanding of value requires similar sophistication in the use of conversion tracking and attribution models. Only when advertisers know both the cost to advertise, on Google, Amazon, Facebook, or elsewhere, and the value produced by these ads in the form of either sales or leads, can they accurately track what truly matters—ROI and profits. In this chapter, we'll explore these opportunities.

With a more complete and nuanced understanding of the best practices that govern the collection and interpretation of data, we'll look at reporting methodologies and identify critical opportunities there for the savvy marketer to outperform the competition.

Attribution models are different methods of explaining how an effect arises from one or more causes. Conversion tracking follows a consumer's path through what was once called the Conversion Funnel but is now more commonly thought of as a multifaceted and complex Consumer Journey.

As the following graphics show, the traditional conversion funnel is linear:

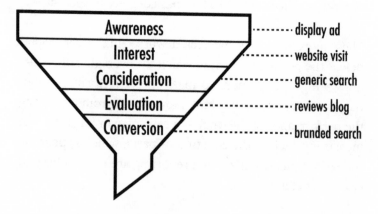

While the Consumer Journey is closer to what probabilists call a "random walk" with users jumping back and forth between different sites and devices and exhibiting a wide range of research behaviors as their interest wanes and peaks based on all the other stimuli they encounter throughout their day.

Let's look at attribution models and conversion tracking as critical areas where an advertiser's human intelligence and business insights can help Google AI do its job better. Again:

HUMANS+ MACHINES > MACHINES ALONE

LESS ACCESS TO DATA

First, let's take a quick overview of the current state of data. The amount of data Google supplies changes constantly. The company has added new capabilities around audience targeting, for example, deepening our understanding through demographics such as age and gender.

But Google has now reduced the amount of information we get about such critical components of the system as search terms. These perpetual changes mean that the best practices of even a year ago may no longer be possible today, or if they are, will be less effective than previously.

Two significant trends are changing the way advertisers interact with data: how much of it is accessible, and how siloed it is. Google collects an enormous amount of data. But, largely motivated by a desire to protect advertisers from being overwhelmed, it has steadily reduced the amount available to advertisers.

Data is becoming more siloed even as it is getting less available. Each platform, from Google to Facebook to Shopify, is a walled garden guarding data on user behavior and preferences that advertisers can only put to use when optimizing that platform.

Data nevertheless remains the currency of the internet. It's the basis for making better decisions about how to pursue a wide range of e-commerce and lead-gen goals.

Average advertisers may indeed be fine with these limitations, much in the way they're happy to let Google AI handle the majority of account management details. The more ambitious advertiser, willing to put in a bit more effort, can still proactively use data—less accessible and increasingly balkanized as it is—to unlevel the playing field.

ATTRIBUTION MODELS

Different attribution models offer different ways of explaining outcomes. For our purposes, "outcomes" means attributing a consumer action—e.g., submitting their contact details in a lead form or checking out their online shopping cart—to their experiences with prior steps in their digital-marketing journey.

Attribution models define digital marketing's value at the various touch points of a consumer's journey towards conversion. As a campaign gets more sophisticated, its attribution model should evolve, too, because an inferior attribution model will lead to an inaccurate assessment of that value. Let's look at a young man's online Adidas sneaker purchase as an example to examine and rank four different attribution models.

Sanjay needs a new pair of sneakers. He's not a brand loyalist, so when he first starts looking around online, he searches only on "sneakers." Google returns a profusion of shopping ads. Sanjay sees a few shoes he likes and makes a mental note of the biggest players in the field—Nike and Adidas.

The next time he searches, Sanjay tries "Nike sneakers" first and then "Adidas sneakers," discovering he prefers what he sees in the second search. He picks out a few models of Adidas sneakers and compares pricing. But he's really just killing time on his phone. When his dinner date shows up, he puts away his phone and forgets about shoes altogether.

A few days later, with some downtime between work meetings, Sanjay goes back to his search. Since only one model has stuck in his mind, he searches "Adidas Ultraboost" and decides that's what he wants. He even picks out the color he likes best. That night, when he gets home, he types in "Adidas Ultraboost men's size 10 black" on his phone and buys his new sneakers.

The following chart compares the four different attribution models we'll consider:

Attribution Models

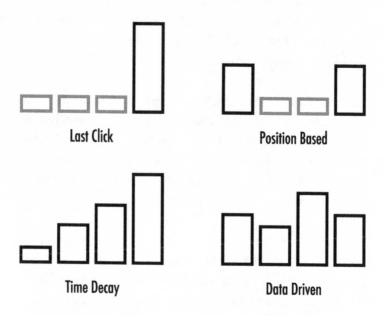

Last Click

Position Based

Time Decay

Data Driven

LAST-CLICK ATTRIBUTION

As mentioned in Chapter 2, the last-click attribution model—Google's default for both Google Ads and Google Analytics—explains a conversion by the last, and only the last, action the user took before converting. The average advertiser may accept this model without question, since any form of measuring conversions correctly is already a huge step up. But more advanced advertisers need to do better. For example, last-click attribution could lead Adidas to conclude that "sneakers" isn't a valuable keyword, even though sneaker sales comprise a considerable portion of its business. To avoid such absurdities, Adidas needs to understand their customers' journey.

Under the last-click attribution model, Sanjay's last, very specific search, "Adidas Ultraboost men's size 10 black," gets full credit for his conversion. Conversely, the keyword "sneakers" isn't even mentioned, as it has virtually no last-click conversions and is much more expensive than Sanjay's last search term.

Even when presented with these arguments, no reasonable digital marketer would turn off a keyword like "sneakers." It's so core to what Adidas sells. You'd know that, although you're not getting many sales directly from it, many customer journeys are likely to start there. Yes, a brand-loyal customer may start with "Adidas," but you're trying to grow your business with new customers, and a broader audience requires being found for generic, nonbrand searches.

The Google Smart Bidding automation doesn't have this insight, as it isn't really very smart. It blindly tries to reach a goal and, if given incomplete information, may well miss the mark.

All Smart Bidding sees is that the advertiser racked up over $10,000 in cost on the keyword "sneakers" and got zero conversions. This looks like a huge waste of money, and it will likely stop bidding on that keyword, potentially making the ad rank so low as to be all but invisible to future sneaker buyers.

POSITION-BASED ATTRIBUTION

Position-based attribution solves the sneaker problem by placing value on the first and last interactions—in Sanjay's case on "sneakers" and "Adidas Ultraboost men's size 10 black." Because it assigns value to the very earliest interaction, those during the awareness-building phase of the funnel or journey, it's a highly effective model for companies that want to be aggressive in building volume, especially with brands that are new or not widely known. An apparel company that started with selling sustainable sneakers like Allbirds, for example, which doesn't yet have the wide name recognition of Adidas or Nike, might want to use position-based attribution.

TIME-DECAY ATTRIBUTION

This model is still more nuanced. Every search is assigned a value whose weight increases the closer it comes to conversion. Sanjay's search for "sneakers" then would register in a way it doesn't under the last-click attribution model, but it would rate as less important than it would under the position-based model. This model includes all the intermediate searches that both the previous models disregarded. This is a great option for more established brands that are looking to maintain their volume rather than grow it aggressively.

Unlike lesser-known brands that can't rely on consumers searching with brand keywords during the consideration phase of a purchase, well-known brands can expect consumers to be aware of and naturally gravitate to researching it beside other options during the research and consideration phase. Anyone who hasn't been living under a rock knows Adidas sells sneakers.

To return to our earlier example, up-and-comer Allbirds isn't as widely known to sell sneakers. So Allbirds would be well served to assign more value to searches during the early, awareness phase for keywords like "sneakers." That way they can introduce themselves to prospective sneaker buyers who never heard of Allbirds.

On the flip side, Adidas can fairly assume that the consumer who just discovered Allbirds may well type in "Adidas newest running shoes" when they get a bit further along the buying journey. It's less important for Adidas to be found on the keyword sneakers than for Allbirds.

This is the power of branding. It helps tremendously even in the PPC world because you don't need to invest as much to get consumers to know you exist and are a trusted vendor in the space.

DATA-DRIVEN ATTRIBUTION

By far the most sophisticated model, data-driven attribution relies on machine learning and thus requires a large number of conversions for training. Google's AI examines the string of searches from initiation to conversion in each individual case. It then compares each search journey's differences and similarities with others to determine the value of each individual search.

Thus, if Sanjay and every other person who ended up buying an Adidas Ultraboost searched "sneakers" and "Adidas" but not "men's size 10" or "black," the category and brand would be weighted more than size and color. Machine learning finds patterns that humans may miss. This is integrated into automated bidding, so that ML can make the best decisions about the bid for every search.

In the example above, searches for "sneakers" and "Adidas" would be considered more desirable, so higher bids will automatically be set by Google's bidding algorithms. "Men's size 10 black," which the machine finds to be a less important search in the journey, would get lower bids to reflect their lesser importance in driving sales. This attribution model gives advertisers most of the data they need to decide how much value to assign to each touchpoint, which can then be fed back into Google.

FROM ATTRIBUTION MODELS TO CONVERSION TRACKING

Even with accelerating PPC automation, conversion tracking and attribution-model selection will remain two incredibly powerful levers for advertisers who want to unlevel the field. Let me explain this using a sports analogy.

Say Steph Curry and his fellow NBA superstars were facing the same existential crisis as us PPC superstars and saw their jobs taken away by automation, or in their case, robots. Programmed with different machine learning models by Coach A and Coach B, how would they get their squads to win the Robot Basketball Association (RBA) championship?

First, in training their machine learning models, the coaches would say the goal of the game is to maximize points, and that points are awarded for putting the ball through the hoop. This is analogous to a conversion in PPC: a basket scored = a conversion.

Now let's look at how different decisions about conversions and attribution models might affect the RBA championship outcome. Coach A informs its players that not all baskets (conversions) are of equal value. They might be one, two, or three points, depending on the type of throw. That is, a value of one, two, or three is assigned to different conversions, depending on the type of conversion.

Coach B, on the other hand, due to an oversight, neglects to mention that not every conversion is of equal value. Its players go into the game believing every basket is worth two points in every circumstance.

The teams now take different approaches on the court. Coach A instructs its players to calculate the probability of making three-pointers and to take a three-point shot only when the odds of sinking one seem favorable. Coach B's players, on the other hand, go for easy shots because they don't know there's a potentially bigger payoff for trying the harder shots from farther away.

In the final seconds, with all the robots but one on each team out of juice, Coach B's team is trailing by three points. Its robot calculates the odds of making two shots but hasn't been programmed to know that one shot is worth three points and the other two. Because the player doesn't know there's a difference in value between the two shots and determines the odds of making the two-point shot are better, it doesn't attempt the three-point shot, which would have forced overtime.

It makes the two-point shot but loses the game. If Google AI doesn't know that some conversions are worth more than others, it'll make you a loser in the largely automated game of PPC. In the robot basketball version of attribution modeling, the coaches record which robot player put the ball through the hoop and which handled the ball beforehand, and then divvy up the value of the points scored between all the robots on the court. Coach B further hamstrings his team by equipping his robot coach with a last-click attribution model, while Coach A uses a time-decay model.

After a few games, the teams start to take very different approaches. Coach B, having noticed that power forwards tend to score the most points, ignores the contributions of other players, and sends out five power forwards every time. Coach A, on the other hand, has learned that certain combinations of players play well together, getting the ball to the best scorer. Its attribution model rewards these nonscoring players for getting the ball into the right hands.

Coach A's team dominates Coach B's because its robots have better data about which conversions matter most and keep the most appropriate goals in mind. They also have an attribution model that better represents the real world, where basketball is a team sport in which fielding five superstars who hate passing can't win as many games as a team that works together.

In PPC, as in robot basketball, savvy operators win by giving machines the best possible information about the path that creates value—attribution—and about what creates the most value—conversion tracking.

LIFETIME AND OMNI-CHANNEL VALUE

As with many aspects of PPC, there isn't a single right answer to tracking and attributing value. What matters most is that advertisers strive for continuous improvement. Eventually this may lead advertisers to add lifetime value and omni-channel performance to how they report conversion value.

For example, a new customer may have spent $100 during a conversion, but the savvy advertiser could report a higher number to Google because their internal models predict this new user will spend another $3,000 on online purchases over the lifetime of the relationship and another $2,000 on in-store purchases.

This is important because the same advertiser will have wildly different abilities to bid and win ad auctions depending on whether they reported $100 of value or $5,100 for acquiring this new customer through PPC. When advertisers wonder why their competition seems to be able to afford really expensive clicks that they themselves can't, it may simply be that the winning advertiser has taken a broader look at the true value of PPC to their business and is winning by better communicating this value to the ad engine.

TRACKING IN A SILOED WORLD

As mentioned earlier, we once understood the path from first contact to sale as a funnel of progressively narrowing searches, from "sneakers" to "Adidas sneakers" to "Adidas Ultraboost size 10." Today, we realize this path is more erratic. Sanjay searched first on his laptop, then his tablet, then at work, and finally at home on his phone. This change in behavior makes it difficult for advertisers to stay in front of potential customers and complicates the task of creating a holistic picture of those customers' journeys.

As we've discussed, new privacy regulations further confound this effort, making it more difficult to track how people jump between devices and channels. Data is also increasingly siloed. Google Ads has data only on the ads a user sees on Google. When a customer goes outside the Google ecosystem into Facebook, for instance, Google can no longer see those steps in the user's journey.

It may even surprise you that, under the new privacy rules, data may not even be shared between two Chrome browsers, even when Google knows the user is logged in on both. For example, in the original FLoC trial, the same user could be assigned to one cohort on their work computer, another on their personal laptop, and yet a third on their smartphone. Data is becoming more siloed, even inside the ad platforms.

A tantalizing prospect is that this may actually help advertisers who've long struggled with showing B2B ads to an audience of business buyers. Say you sell heavy-duty deep fryers for professional kitchens. How do you ensure your ad isn't seen by someone like me: a Belgian who by some sort of unwritten law must own and keep a deep fryer in their house? (Go ahead. Next time you meet a Belgian, ask if they own a deep fryer.) Today, that's very difficult because it's relatively hard to target a consumer (B2C) versus a business (B2B) audience. In a world where a person can be in different cohorts based on what device they're using, it's possible to imagine it being easier to instruct Google to show ads to a B2B audience when they search "deep fryer."

As data from the ad platforms and third parties you work with becomes harder to access, think of ways to better leverage your own first-party data. Once a customer lands on your site, with their permission, you can collect their data regardless of its originating channel. The relationship shifts from third to first party. You can then use Google Analytics or other measurement and reporting systems to look across channels and gain insights that the engines themselves can't provide.

For example, you can see the same user first came through an Instagram ad, then a Google ad, and finally from an email you sent them before they made a purchase. Instagram, Google, and your email marketing manager will all claim credit for that conversion because they live in their own silos. Thanks to the data you collected in Google Analytics, you can understand all three share the credit, and none should get all.

You can then act on that data, for example, by adjusting your budgets for Google Ads to factor in that part of your budget should be reserved for Instagram and email blasts. Bringing additional information into Google from outside its ecosystem to inform it of your company's unique needs is a prime practice for unleveling the playing field. Google, after all, has no idea what, if any, data from outside its ecosystem might be relevant to your business. Nor does it know what information you need to report to stakeholders.

GOOGLE CLICK ID (GCLID)

Google Click ID is another tool in the sophisticated PPC practitioner's arsenal to help with conversion reporting. It assigns a unique identifier, a Google Click ID (GCLID), to every ad shown in the system. Now, every new click that lands on your website arrives with a record in its URL tracking string of where it comes from. An advertiser can use that string as a unique key to connect Google's data with their own, giving the AI system a leg up in determining which users and circumstances are most likely to convert.

Take a look at the following screenshot of an AdWords API report. Advertisers can find a great deal of data in Google Ads API reports that isn't readily available in the Google Ads interface. In this example, we've looked up the Click Performance Report, which stores data associated with the GCLID.

An advertiser who records nothing but the GCLID when a user visits their landing page from a click on a Google ad can now find out much more about that click: the exact ad seen; how the user was targeted, e.g., with a keyword or a placement; where the user was located; and much more.

Examples of data available for every ad click in the Click Performance Report:

- Ad format (text, video, image, etc.)
- Location of interest
- Location where the search originated
- Whether an ad was part of an ad variation experiment
- Click Type (main ad, extension, call, etc.)
- Keyword or placement
- Audience

- Device (desktop, mobile, connected TV, etc.,)
- Keyword match type
- On what page of the results the ad was clicked
- Slot (top of page, other, etc.)

GOOGLE ADS API REPORTS

Not only can you access your account's Google Ads API Reports—you should! These reports contain far more information than is available on your account's front end, some of which will be able to give you a competitive edge.

These reports aren't sent to you automatically. You have to request them or use a script I wrote that automatically pulls the reports up.

I strongly advocate taking this more proactive approach to your account data. It can help you strike pay dirt.

GCLIDs can also help advertisers account for sales resulting from their salespeople's off-line efforts. The GCLID of a potential customer's first click on an ad can be captured in a hidden field automatically inserted into a lead-gen form that becomes part of your CRM system.

Every interaction, online or off, incorporated into the CRM record will then be linked to that individual's customer journey—especially the interaction associated with conversion, the action that turns a prospective customer into an actual one.

This wealth of information helps you tie conversions to specific search terms, keywords, ads, and campaigns. Google can further tie this to the hundreds of thousands of additional attributes of the search and armed with that data, preferentially bid more in the future for similar types of clicks that tend to lead to sales.

DATA: MORE CAN BE MORE

Google doesn't have any idea what other data might be relevant to calculating your ads' CPC. It won't get the weather forecast for Alonzo and increase his bids for car battery ads after a freeze. Alonzo—or his agency—has to do that himself.

Likewise, Stan, an online stockbroker, might be fully aware that he's more likely to sign up new retail investors when there is a bull market, and everyone has a friend who seems to be making a killing on stocks or cryptocurrency. But his Google Ads account has no idea of this requirement or when it is met. If it were properly informed, his bids could be adjusted accordingly. Likewise, Carrie, the recruiter, might import employment data, and Deidre, a travel agent, could bring in data about the locations and dates of festivals and celebrations.

What external or publicly available data would unlevel the playing field for you? Sometimes, this is perfectly obvious. More frequently, PPC advertisers aren't entirely sure what data points are the most meaningful. Unsure what data is most relevant, the average marketer will only track a limited number of inputs.

But those limits can be both self-imposed and arbitrary. ML automations offer you the ability to use as much data as you wish to give you an edge. And this is true even if you don't know the exact factors the machines may already be looking at.

As another example, let's say that Quinten invented a new

kind of glass cleaner that doesn't leave streaks when you wash your windows in the bright sun. He took it on *Shark Tank*, and QVC added it to their inventory. QVC has access to a tremendous amount of data including the time Quinten's spots air, who's hosting, whether the host is male or female, and potentially hundreds of additional public and proprietary data points.

The average marketer would be completely overwhelmed if they tried to track every possibly relevant data point—any human would be—but this is where machine learning shines. For ML, there's no such thing as "too much data."

Of course, it's possible to go overboard. The more data you bring in, the bigger your data sets become, which will increase how much it costs and how long it takes to run each analysis. Nevertheless, using machine intelligence to filter potentially relevant data can yield any number of insights. For example, QVC might learn that the gender of the host has a huge impact on how many people buy Quinten's glass cleaner. Who knew?

Say you think something has an impact on your ads' performance, but you're not sure what. The strategy of bringing in a great deal of data and letting Google ML sift it for patterns can give you a significant edge.

REPORTING

Advertisers must also separate the nitty-gritty data needed for day-to-day management from that which will most effectively demonstrate their value to executives, clients, and other stakeholders. Good reporting translates raw data into documents and dashboards that clearly demonstrate performance.

Typically, when PPC professionals talk about reporting, they refer to the type of high-level overviews they need to send to clients or company executives. The focus is on internal reporting.

These reports' stated purpose is usually to update recipients on digital-marketing performance. But clients and executives don't just want to see data. They want your interpretation of it, which can be trickier.

Anyone would be delighted to hear they sold 10 percent more this month than last. But this news will be more actionable if you can explain how Google Ads AI, with your help, achieved that result. If action-oriented RSA messaging that focused on a "buy online, pick up in-store" (BOPIS) option was responsible for the improved performance, it's critical to share this insight if you want your business partners to agree to continuing this strategy.

If its marketing department were able to tell Shoes Unlimited executives that blue Nikes don't sell as well as black ones online, they will have supplied an insight that could influence the company's business strategy to market in the coming year: market black Nikes more aggressively!

Similarly, an analysis of which search terms are driving success can be valuable to stakeholders not directly involved in PPC marketing. For example, the SEO team might decide to prioritize some keywords that have huge potential but are underperforming. Assuming blue hasn't become an untrendy color, there's no reason blue sneakers shouldn't be attracting attention, if underperforming keywords were replaced with more effective ones. Or the production team could use this data to right-size their order for the next shipment from its factory in China. Thanks to the speed and relative transparency of PPC, this can be a great source of insights for the whole company and make you, the PPC team, look like superheroes.

STATIC VS. ACTIVE

Monthly reports, when delivered either as a PDF or in the body of an email, are static. Whether executives or the client look at them on the day they arrive or wait until the end of the year, the report will be the same. This is ideal if the report includes your insights. After all, it would be awkward to send a client a note, with a link to live data, saying how great their campaign is performing, and three weeks later, when they finally open the report, see the performance is much worse and think you didn't know what you were talking about.

Data in active or live reports updates in real time and can be very useful, too. Three of the most relevant types of active reporting are dashboards, spreadsheets, and visualizations.

Dashboards, which are regularly updated, provide real-time information, which is much more valuable than a static report in helping account-management teams identify anomalies that need immediate attention.

Spreadsheet-based reports are almost exclusively relevant to account managers. They capture a tremendous amount of detail and provide performance data on every campaign, keyword, geographic location, and other parameters.

Data visualization can be illustrated with Optmyzr's PPC

Investigator. It illustrates both how and why conversions change from one period to the next. Using this tool enables advertisers to compare, for example, this month's conversions to the same month's last year.

Data Visualizations

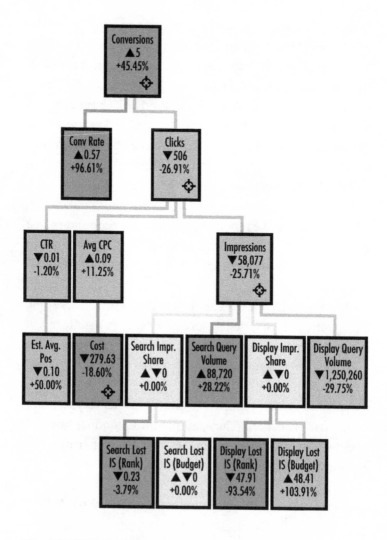

Say conversions are up 20 percent. That's great! But why? To uncover the cause, you'll need to track every step that leads to a conversion. First, an ad must appear in response to a potential customer's search. Then, the ad needs to be compelling enough to entice that user to click. Finally, the offer needs to be convincing enough that the user converts.

Impressions lead to clicks. Clicks lead to conversions.

The PPC Investigator identifies where in that process something changed, which then increased the number of conversions. If there is a 20 percent increase in conversions, it might be because a higher percentage of clicks convert. Or the conversion-rate percentage might have stayed the same, but the number of initial clicks has gone up. Or maybe more people saw the ad in the first place because of an external factor, such as weather or time of year, which boosted interest in a certain type of product.

An increase anywhere along the path will have the same result in the end. But knowing the root cause of a change in conversion numbers will help you further unlevel the playing field, because you now know how to maximize the opportunity.

ALERTS

Alerts are an ideal automation layer that will quickly let PPC pilots know when an automation goes haywire.

Automation is great when applied as one part of a more strategic approach to solving society's needs. But it isn't foolproof or perfect. And it doesn't fully take into account all variables, particularly intangibles. Which means, don't mistake automation for autopilot. By last count, at least Tesla drivers wish they'd better understood this difference.

The machines are getting smarter, but machine learning and artificial intelligence are *not* any of the following:

- Artificial intuition
- Artificial intellect
- Artificial improvisation
- Artificial insight

Humans possess those essential traits of intuition, intellect, improvisational flair, and insight, so humans still play the pivotal role in paid search. Sure, it's possible to create functional, competent PPC by putting things essentially on autopilot. But who wants to just be functional?

Great PPC is there for the taking, but it requires PPC pros who want to use autopilot for what it's good for, allowing them to remain captains of the PPC airliner.

As the pilot in command, the PPC pro needs to monitor all systems—exploring every nuance of their programs. They need to look beneath the surface information, because the myriad automations built by the ad engines can only take them so far toward their true goals.

Custom alerts like those found in Optmyzr have expanded greatly, particularly over the last year or so. They generally can be categorized into five levels:

1. Account-level alerts can help prioritize time allocation, for example, by working first on accounts that are missing their target conversion volumes by the greatest margins.
2. Campaign-level alerts, launched in 2020, can surface opportunities to make even well-performing accounts do even better, for example, by pointing to a campaign that's dragging down account averages.
3. Label-level alerts help monitor multiple campaigns with a common theme, such as brand campaigns or campaigns for specific product lines. By looking at this level, you can discover performance anomalies for all campaigns associated with home appliances, for instance, or how all campaigns associated with a brand such as Adidas are doing.
4. Bid-strategy-level alerts allow monitoring performance of campaigns whose bids are automatically managed by the ad engine. They will let you know whether Smart Bidding campaigns are hitting the mark or not.
5. Budget-level alerts help advertisers spend their whole budget without overspending on individual accounts, a specific set of campaigns, or many accounts across all platforms, including Google, Microsoft, Facebook, and Amazon. Knowing when you're depleting an overall budget across these four engines can be complicated because you have to pull that data from four different places. An automation layer is particularly helpful because it can stay on top of that for you.

AUTOMATING REPORTS

Producing reports is one of the biggest drains on a PPC marketing professional's time. I've seen many agencies spend days at the beginning of every month going through their data—pulling and massaging it—to generate the reports their clients expect. This process is both inefficient and prone to the errors and omissions that contribute to client churn.

At a minimum, advertisers should have that data automatically put in place for them. Simple and effective free scripts can pull data from Google Ads, put it into a spreadsheet, and keep it updated automatically. This will ensure you always have the latest available data. Here's how to access some of these:

**Find Resources
Related to This Book At:**
https://www.optmyzr.com/books/unlevel/

Additional automation layers can set up triggers to alert you when immediate attention is required. Others can compare one week's results against another's.

For example, when some unforeseen, newsworthy event occurs, you could find trending search terms that went from very low to high impression levels. This data could help identify new opportunities, such as the need for a new ad more relevant to the trending keyword. Or the need for negative keywords in trending searches too loosely related to an advertiser's offer.

Take a look at the following graphic from Google Trends:

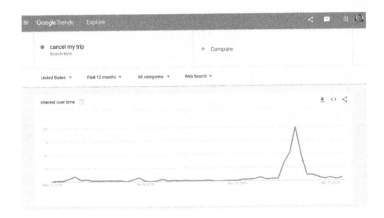

Generally, the keyword "cancel my trip" has extremely low search volume. Except for the months when the COVID-19 pandemic first hit. The total amount of money spent on that keyword is normally negligible but during those months tens of thousands of dollars might be spent on it unnecessarily. After all, no advertiser wants to pay for a click that helps a consumer get a refund.

Automation layers can help you take advantage of the enormous amount of online data that ad systems generate. For a human, pulling and analyzing data from a large set of search terms and multiple sources over different date ranges would be overwhelming. But apps like Optmyzr's Conversion Lasso, for example, can almost instantaneously do a deep analysis of many reports and recommend new keywords based on your account's performance. Automated reporting ensures that those insights will remain top of mind and actionable.

To repeat Peter Drucker's well-known maxim: "If you can't

measure it, you can't improve it." Attribution modeling and conversion tracking are critical data-measurement sources that automation layering will help you mine more effectively. The same is true of reporting, with automation layering enabling you to save data-collection time that can then be applied to critical analysis.

And there's another data source that's particularly important to decision-making: that which comes from experimentation.

CHAPTER 8

· · · ·

EXPERIMENTATION

Google and Microsoft constantly bombard advertisers with tales of the extraordinary results purportedly generated by their newest features and capabilities. How does the savvy marketer decide which automations to use?

You can't simply ask Google or imitate your peers. Nor can you necessarily look to successful accounts you've managed in the past.

Often, it's the process around a capability rather than any particular feature or automation that generated those great results. Both Walmart and Target offer a buy-online-pickup-in-store (BOPIS) option. Target had curbside customer service manned by employees with bespoke iPhone apps and a goal to deliver orders in under three minutes. Walmart forced customers to go to the returns desk, wait in line, and then wait some more for the guest service rep to find the purchase in a cluttered back room. Two implementations of the same idea, but guess which one performed better? It's not the idea that was broken; it was the execution.

The only way to confidently attribute an outcome to a particular factor, such as a new automation, is to experiment. But you need to pick the right experimental framework for each test. Broadly speaking, there are three options, all of which rest on the comparison of a control to the results of the experiment: time-based tests, market-split tests, and cookie-split tests.

TIME-BASED TESTS

In the days before search engines had built-in experimentation tools, time-based or before-and-after tests were the standard. These are the simplest kind of experimentation. The control scenario is a period of time before which the change to be tested is made. In theory, with all other factors held as constant as possible and the only difference between the control (or before) and experiment (or after) scenarios being the change to be tested, any difference in outcome can be attributed to the experimental change.

Bernard's agency wants to test one of Google's new automations for another of his agency's clients, a gourmet gift company. He meets with his staff to discuss this initiative. They know better than to blindly believe the new technology will automatically be better than their current approach. They decide to run an experiment to test the validity of the premise that this new automation will be an improvement.

Since it's November 15, Bernard proposes using the past two weeks—November 1–14—as his control. He plans to implement the change today and, on November 30, compare the second two-week period—November 16–30—with the first.

I've worked in PPC for over twenty years and know very well

it's ridiculous to propose an e-commerce company would even dare to run an experiment in this particular time frame or almost any other time in Q4. In fact, while I worked at Google, there was a virtual moratorium on any noncritical product launches in ads for fear of creating waves, or worse, breaking a finely prepared advertiser campaign at its moment of truth for the year, Black Friday. But stick with me, as these dates are the clearest way to illustrate my point.

The problem, one of Bernard's associates points out to his embarrassment, is that Black Friday and Cyber Monday will skew the results. Bernard could wait a month, but the holiday season will then be in full force. Even if he waits to run his test until the first month without a major holiday, he knows there's no way to predict if other world events might taint his results.

This is an inherent flaw in time-based experiments. On the other hand, they're inexpensive to run, easy to set up, and can test almost any alteration Bernard might think of, including a new automation.

MARKET-SPLIT TESTS

Where a time-based experiment tests an experimental change across all targeted users, regardless of where they are located, a market-split test looks at how it would affect different markets. It applies the experimental condition to one market and compares outcomes with those of a control.

The national market can be split—e.g., north versus south or east versus west—or the split can focus on two submarkets, most typically two similar cities. Seattle and Portland are frequently used as an example for this kind of testing because—and no offense to either for the comparison—they're quite a lot alike. They're both located in the Northwest with populations of similar size and demographics.

Having rejected time-based testing as having too many variables he can't control, Bernard decides to run a market-split test, experimenting with bidding strategy. Using Portland as his control, he sets up his experiment to run in Seattle.

If, two weeks later, when he looks at his results, he sees that sales in Portland have gone up by 10 percent, and Seattle by 15 percent, Bernard can safely attribute that additional 5 percent increase to his change in bidding strategy. If, on the other hand, Portland is up by 10 percent and Seattle by only 5, he will probably revert to his original strategy.

Market-split tests are only feasible for larger companies. A small online retailer who only sells a few hundred dollars' worth of product a week won't have a large enough sample size in each of two markets to make this kind of test meaningful.

COOKIE-SPLIT TESTS

Most major ad engines like Google and Microsoft now have their own native experimentation framework. Google's, called "Drafts and Experiments," allows advertisers to create a draft campaign that includes the change they'd like to test and to set a percentage of traffic to direct to the experiment rather than the control. Most advertisers elect to go with a fifty–fifty split. Google uses cookies to manage splitting the audience and directing half each to the campaign's experimental and control versions.

Google doesn't simply divide the searches by sending every

other one to the experimental site. To increase the likelihood of a true "apples-to-apples" comparison, the split is randomized. For each new search, Google essentially flips a coin and directs the traffic accordingly. The laws that govern probability ensure that, although three searches in a row might go to the same campaign, a random choice between two options will evenly split the traffic over time.

Google's cookies also ensure continuity of user experience. A user who enters the same search a day later will be deliberately steered to the same version of the campaign to which they were first directed randomly.

Despite its elegance, Google's Drafts and Experiments framework has some downsides. Google limits the changes advertisers can make, and the framework can't entirely control for outside variables. Then again, no test can.

I've seen the same ad inside the same ad group with the same text, keywords, and bids, running simultaneously return different results. An A/B test of the exact same ad can result in a statistically significant winner because there will always be things out of your control that affect the outcome.

Yes, you heard right. Even if you do an ad test where the new ad is exactly the same as the old ad, you may find a winner and loser even though there is no difference between them.

This is because of differences among the users who saw the ad. Perhaps someone started her search predisposed to buy, while another arrived at the company site by mistake. The advertiser who understands these limitations will be better positioned to avoid embarrassing mistakes.

TEST EVALUATION

A very granular campaign structure such as GRIP, discussed in Chapter 6, can ameliorate some of these issues. But such structures often require additional measurements that must be planned for. Again, a great place to get this data is from your Google API reports.

To evaluate an A/B test properly, the advertiser must work with their data to make it as much an apples-to-apples comparison as possible. Rather than simply comparing the metrics of two ad variations in the same ad group, the advertiser should build a data map with all known factors related to ad auctions. This includes the search term, the location, the position of the ad, the device type, the audience, and more.

This map in hand, the trick is to find similar segments that triggered different ad variations at a high enough frequency to allow for a statistically sound determination of a winner and a loser. This process is not simple. If it were, all advertisers would do it. But with a good automation layer, the process becomes manageable and can give you an unfair edge over your competition.

The following is a graphic of a data map of this kind:

Ad Group

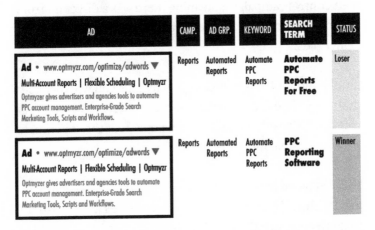

Ad • www.optmyzr.com/optimize/adwords ▼
Multi-Account Reports | Flexible Scheduling | Optmyzr
Optmyzer gives advertisers and agencies tools to automate
PPC account management. Enterprise-Grade Search Marketing
Tools, Scripts and Workflows.

WINNER

Ad • www.optmyzr.com/optimize/adwords ▼
Multi-Account Reports | Flexible Scheduling | Optmyzr
Optmyzer gives advertisers and agencies tools to automate
PPC account management. Enterprise-Grade Search Marketing
Tools, Scripts and Workflows.

LOSER

An A/B ad test in an ad group can reveal that two identical copies of an ad could win and lose at the same time.

AD	CAMP.	AD GRP.	KEYWORD	SEARCH TERM	STATUS
Ad • www.optmyzr.com/optimize/adwords ▼ Multi-Account Reports | Flexible Scheduling | Optmyzr Optmyzer gives advertisers and agencies tools to automate PPC account management. Enterprise-Grade Search Marketing Tools, Scripts and Workflows.	Reports	Automated Reports	Automate PPC Reports	**Automate PPC Reports For Free**	Loser
Ad • www.optmyzr.com/optimize/adwords ▼ Multi-Account Reports | Flexible Scheduling | Optmyzr Optmyzer gives advertisers and agencies tools to automate PPC account management. Enterprise-Grade Search Marketing Tools, Scripts and Workflows.	Reports	Automated Reports	Automate PPC Reports	PPC **Reporting Software**	Winner

By building a data map with additional details, like what search term triggered the ad, we can start to understand that whether the ad wins or loses has nothing to do with the ad copy, but everything to do with the different search term variations the ad is shown for.

There can also be unpredictable second-order effects. The simple act of running an experiment changes the advertising ecosystem. And how your competitors respond to your experiment can have impact across the board, not just in the area you're testing.

One of our customers had just such an experience while testing Smart Bidding across a subset of their campaigns. Those campaigns did well, but the campaigns in the control group started suffering large losses in impression share.

Digging into the data made it clear that Google had raised the CPCs for the Smart Bidding campaigns. Competitors noticed and responded by raising their own bids across the board. These higher bids were often for keywords our client had in their control campaigns, meaning there was a direct hit from the unintended consequences of forcing competitors to make higher bids.

Another downside is that Google only tells you whether your draft experimental campaign out- or underperformed your control. It doesn't pinpoint which portion of the experiment was responsible for its success.

The average advertiser will be satisfied with having identified a winner. But if you want to outcompete, there's an opportunity to go deeper into the data to discover what portions of the experiment were responsible for the improvement.

Take Bernard's agency and his client Betty's Blooms. Bernard wants to experiment with new keywords and adds "bouquet of roses" to the account. Google, using the same close variant technique that supplemented "floral arrangements" with "arranging flowers," now includes "rose bouquets," "vase of roses," and other phrases it considers relevant, showing Bernard's ads for them all.

There were suddenly more purchases of expensive rose bouquets delivered overnight. Better yet, many customers made the upsell purchase of a glass vase or bowl. An average advertiser would be perfectly content with this experiment and keep "roses" as a keyword.

But Bernard wants to unlevel the playing field. He conducts a query analysis and discovers that for the new keyword "bouquet of roses," Google is serving up Bernard's ad in response to the search "rose bowl." People entering that term are almost certainly looking for something else entirely—probably a football game or the famous Sunday swap meet.

The agency introduces "-rose bowl" as a negative keyword. A less diligent agency, seeing only the aggregate increase, would not have noticed the wasted ad spend on "rose bowl," and Google would not have surfaced it on its own.

Google's Drafts and Experiments framework is quite good at returning a verdict on which of the halves of a cookie-split test performs better. But as Bernard saw, an overall, winner-and-loser description of an experiment's outcome is partial at best. At a less diligent agency, "bouquet of roses" would have looked like a 100 percent win, even though it wasn't.

The opposite scenario is yet more dangerous. Too often, the

average advertiser will conduct an experiment on a tool like automated bidding, see their performance go down, and conclude the tool doesn't work for them. You always need to dig deeper and look at why the experiment returned the results it did.

It's easy for automated bidding to fail if an advertiser, who might want to brush up on his PPC doctor skills, hasn't gotten all the prerequisites in place. For example, did the advertiser set up conversion reporting correctly, ideally weighting the values of different types of conversion? Did they select a good attribution model, rather than last-click? Did they maintain good account hygiene with consistent structure, good targeting, and negative keywords?

A lazy experiment will confirm that there are no silver bullets in PPC. But that doesn't mean performance can't be improved with effort correctly applied.

MORE EXPERIMENTS

Bernard has been doing manual bidding and wants to continue doing so. But he thinks his CPA (cost per acquisition) is too high. As an experiment, he decides to use a lower bid, and discovers that his CPA has gone up. He's spending less per click, but more per new customer.

If Bernard were an average advertiser, that would be it. He'd conclude the experiment didn't work and keep on doing things the old way—which is what he really wanted to do in the first place.

But Bernard also wants to develop an unfair advantage. Looking deeper, digging down to a more granular view, he sees that by lowering his bids, he's no longer comparing apples to apples. Because he was bidding less, his ads were no longer competing in top-tier auctions. He got the same number of clicks and paid less for them, but they were originating from lower-quality searches, which led to fewer conversions. The problem was somewhat similar to the mortgage form-fills for Betty's bank.

Bernard is now able to see that he has choices beyond the obvious one of reverting to his previous strategy. He can keep his bids low and get very aggressive about putting in negative keywords, doing something similar to what he did for Betty's Blooms by ruling out "rose bowl" as a search term.

Alternately, Bernard might experiment with raising his bid to be more competitive in the better auctions. His goal, remember, is not to bid less per click, but to spend less per acquisition. Paying more for fewer bids of higher quality might lower his CPA, just as paying less per bid increased what he paid for each acquisition.

Bernard's approach allows him to maximize his experiments' benefits and, consequently, those of every new automation and innovation he implements. Or it would if he weren't now completely swamped with having to check each week for new, underperforming close variants that should become negative keywords. Fortunately, again, automation layering can help keep the gains that such labor-intensive work yields, while significantly diminishing the actual labor.

Google gives users several ways to automate requests for reports that are more granular than those it sends automatically. Advertisers can even put push notifications in place for certain subsets of data that they want to watch more closely.

This kind of automation layer is easy to set in the Google interface. While such automations tend to look at very simple conditions, they can be quite helpful and cost nothing.

More advanced automation layers can help advertisers dig more deeply into the results of their experiments to further unlevel the playing field. Let's take a look.

When Bernard experiments with RSAs (responsive search ads), his client is thrilled with the results. But he isn't satisfied to simply reap the rewards. He wants to understand what caused them.

Bernard is interested in discovering what new searches the automation had made his client eligible for. RSAs dynamically construct ads from components on the fly at every auction, creating ads that are more relevant than static ones. Thanks to this enhanced relevance, Google may now be able to show the ad for searches where the Quality Score was previously too low. As a result, using RSAs can increase the search terms an advertiser is eligible to show ads for.

Looking at the most granular data for each query would be extraordinarily time-consuming and tedious. Using an automation layer to filter the results of his experiment, Bernard discovers a fantastic query that his old-school ads didn't qualify for. In fact, it was one that had never occurred to him.

The unlikely but effective search term was "cat-safe flower bouquets," meaning bouquets that don't contain potentially poisonous plants such as poinsettias. This ad was shown for the query because the RSA combined titles and descriptions focused on sustainability and eco-friendly packaging to achieve a high enough Quality Score so the ad could be shown to the concerned pet lover.

Bernard splits the query "cat-safe flower bouquets" out and makes it a specifically targeted keyword, along with a great relevant ad and landing page. All of this grows his client's business incrementally, especially during the Christmas season.

Without an automation layer to guide Bernard to this discovery and help him capitalize on it, his client would still have been happy. Not content to settle for the average advertiser's high-level analysis of an experiment's results, however, Bernard was able to gain an almost user-by-user understanding of what compels his client's users to convert.

PART 2 SUMMARY

METHODOLOGY

Sophisticated deployment of three digital marketing methodologies—Campaign Structure, Measurement, and Experimentation—is critical for unleveling the playing field to your advantage.

Google Ads AI enables a much greater variety of campaign structures than previously. It works with both less and more granular structures. When greater granularity is introduced to support business goals that Google machine learning may have no inkling about, fantastic results can follow. And granularity doesn't have to be massively complicated to manage if you use technology to your advantage and create your own automation layers on top of the engines' ML automations.

Granularity should not be a dirty word in the age of automated PPC. The right granularity can be the thing that sets your campaign apart from all those who are happy to just let Google control everything. Ease of use is great in the abstract, but a little more work can often yield far superior results.

That being said, one size does not fit all. Not every campaign benefits from this kind of micromanagement. It's often appropriate to employ a less granular structure through grouping products by category, geography, profit margin, and budget allocation.

Go granular when advisable. But don't go hypergranular when you can get the desired results more simply.

Ad customizers, for example, are automation layers that can provide a more granular level of control within less granular structures. On the other hand, if you are using Smart Bidding, a highly granular SKAG structure may be the most viable option.

It bears repeating: there is no such thing as a perfect campaign structure, but there is one that's best for your business. Only you have to tailor it yourself.

Measurement is a second critical methodology for unleveling the playing field and serves as the basis for attribution models and conversion tracking. Today, users' journeys are more complicated than ever, with interactions on multiple devices, visits to more sites and apps, and more time spent researching across a variety of channels, including social, video, and search. So, understanding the "customer journey" and using that data to optimize can have a big impact.

The four most commonly encountered attribution models are:

1. Last-click attribution: the default but also the least helpful.

2. Position-based attribution: which evaluates first and last interactions.
3. Time-decay attribution: which takes account of the entire customer journey, with each successive interaction considered more valuable than the last.
4. Data-driven attribution: a machine-learning-based model that is the most nuanced of the four.

Attribution models work hand-in-hand with conversion tracking to help deliver more leads and sales. In general, the more data AI has to analyze, the more accurate such models become. It is particularly useful to integrate the data generated outside the ads' ecosystem—whether on different platforms or non-digitally—into conversion reporting. For machine learning, there is no such thing as too much data, and the insights gained are critical for outmaneuvering the competition.

These analyses then become the basis for internal reporting, which at its best concerns not only the what of a certain outcome but the why. Compiling reports can be exceedingly time-consuming. Automating reports to the greatest possible extent will enable marketers to focus on explaining, rather than detailing, outcomes.

Experimentation is a third, critical methodology for capturing an unfair advantage. Such experiments compare a control with a campaign with one changed factor or parameter.

The three experimental frameworks are:

1. Time-based: with a simple "before" and "after" structure, with the "before" (often a current campaign) being the control and the "after" testing the results of a single change.

2. Market-split: which splits a campaign into generally similar markets, such as Portland and Seattle, using one as the control and the other as the experiment.
3. Cookie-split: which uses cookies to split the campaigns into control and experiment, often using a randomization process.

You can't take the results of such tests at face value. Dig further to find the reasons behind the results before deciding whether and how to change your campaign.

With these three methodologies in place, you will be well-positioned to step fully into your new role as strategist and begin implementation of the automation layering and other strategies that will unlevel the playing field exponentially in your favor.

To help you do so, let's take a look at where the rubber meets the road: implementation strategies.

IMPLEMENTATION

CHAPTER 9

.
.
.
.

STRATEGIC AUTOMATION LAYERING

The aim of the strategies in this book is to exert greater control over Google Ads machine learning, while maintaining as much ease of use as possible. The purpose of exerting greater control is, as always, to increase profitability. And to do so in a way that frees up your time from rote work, enabling you, in the strategist role, to develop tactics that will continue to unlevel the playing field and beat the competition.

In Part 3, we'll look at specific implementations of these types of strategy, which involve automation layering, becoming a Google Ads power user, or both. Here's where the rubber meets the road. We'll be looking at a number of different strategies that all come under the rubric of the "right audience for the right bid with the right message." That is: strategic targeting, bidding, and messaging.

Beforehand, we'll look at the bigger picture of how these strategies can be implemented and deployed. There are four options:

1. Become a power user of Google's built-in tools.
2. Use third-party scripts.
3. Use third-party automation tools.
4. Employ a development team to work with the Google API (Application Programming Interface).

These options range from less to more complex. But more complex does not necessarily mean better. If a simpler solution does the trick, great.

POWER USER: GOOGLE'S BUILT-IN TOOLS

Google's engineers have methodically built an automated ad system that, for all its virtues, ultimately works on a one-size-fits-all basis. The underlying message is, "Hand control over to us. We'll optimize results while making your life much easier."

As you've seen, such "optimization" only goes so far. It's fine for the run-of-the-mill advertiser, but you don't want to be run of the mill. To rise above the pack, you need to tweak the system.

This game's first level is becoming a power user of Google's built-in tools. In many cases, the Google automated ad system allows for changing and adjusting parameters, and Google offers automated rules that enable you to refine what you want to automate.

Something as simple as an automated monitor-and-report

function—consisting of monitoring an account for certain conditions and sending you, as the PPC pilot, an alert when they arise—can be incredibly useful.

For example, Bernard's agency might decide to experiment with automated bidding for its Betty's Blooms account, establishing a tCPA of $25. He uses a portfolio strategy applicable for multiple campaigns that allows for some variation in CPA, as long as the average stays around $25.

But this leaves Bernard open to the portfolio effect, in which an overall average hides critical details. Google will only show him how the bid strategy is doing, which might hide some expensive keywords or an ad group driving conversions at $100 each.

However, by making some simple adjustments to the system, Bernard can set an alert to monitor components of the overall portfolio and send a notification if, for example, a specific keyword spends more than a set amount for an acquisition. To increase control, Bernard could and should look at not only summary reports but the Google campaign- and ad-group reports that are available on request. Being proactive will yield superior results.

One of the biggest limitations of Google's built-in tools is that Google decides what's permissible. For example, they discourage SKAGs, which we discussed earlier, so there's no easy way to create them in the Google Ads interface. Third-party tools and automation layers you create yourself leave the choice in your hands. Optmyzr, for example, supports easy creation of SKAGs. If you've decided they're right for your account, we'll make it easy for you to turn that decision into action.

IMPORTED SCRIPTS

In the early days, customization was entirely a DIY proposition. People, including me, built small scripts to solve issues we had with the Google AdWords system. We then shared these customizations, posting them on sites, like *Search Engine Land*, *Search Engine Journal*, and *PPC Hero*, for anyone who wanted to use them to solve a similar problem. The practice continues today.

These free scripts are easily available. You can go online, search for the problem you've encountered, and append "Google ad script" to your query. In many cases, you'll find a script that deals with the issue, which you can then copy and paste into your Google Ads account free of charge. A pseudocode (that is, plain English) example of such a script would be: *If* more than twenty-four hours elapse without Google showing my ad, *then* send me an email alert.

A preexisting script may need to be modified to address your problem more precisely. This means making changes to the code. Perhaps the only thing you need to change is the numbers of the smartphones to which text alerts are sent.

But, as those with some coding experience know, even here, a single mistake in the address array, a forgotten comma or extra space, can keep the script from working properly. For advertisers who never had a coding class, hiring a programmer to rework a script's code is a solid option. Obviously, it's critical that the coder you hire is a Google Ads expert who understands what you're trying to accomplish.

There is one additional complication when importing scripts. About three times a year, Google changes how its scripts and

API work. Each time they do, you or your coder may have to go in and update all your imported scripts to keep them from breaking. But better this than having to make daily or even hourly manual adjustments.

THIRD-PARTY, OFF-THE-SHELF TOOLS

Third-party, off-the-shelf tools like Optmyzr's pick up where Google's built-in ones leave off. They're also the evolutionary successor of DIY scripts downloaded from the internet. These tools aren't free, but they don't require the user to have any coding chops or to hire someone who does.

Perhaps the single most impactful advantage a third-party tool gives its users is the ability to automate importing and using their own business data to optimize an account. Alonzo, for example, can't create different campaigns for his auto parts based on their different margins because he can't currently import profitability numbers into his Google Ads account. That's because Google doesn't have a field for storing profits, only a field for conversion value.

Third-party tools bridge that gap. The right automation layer will make it simple to import business data and then combine it with data from the Google Ads system to formulate and implement advanced strategies.

Bernard, as a power user, tweaked one of Google's simple automations to monitor his $25 tCPA. If he decides he wants to find not just those ad groups that are already missing the target, but also those trending towards missing the target soon, he's out of luck. Google limits him to checking on his accounts for a single date range, for example, by analyzing what happened over the past week. But trend analysis requires looking at multiple date ranges, and Google doesn't support this in their automated rules.

A third-party tool like Optmyzr gives Bernard the option of searching over multiple date ranges and incorporating his own business data to set thresholds. The aim is to create sophisticated alerts that compare performance changes over a span of several weeks. This enables him to find an ad group that's meeting the $25 CPA, but that has been on a four-week decline and will probably miss the target next week unless corrective action is taken.

With that information, Bernard can go into the Google system and make adjustments. Or he could automate those as well, constructing an automation layer that monitors and adjusts according to his business logic. It then presents him with a single one-click "I approve these changes" button. Because you only have to set parameters and conditions once to have them applied indefinitely, such a third-party automation layer is an enormous time-saver and stress-reducer because a lot of peace of mind comes with knowing your own automation is monitoring what Google does with your ads.

Over at the recruitment agency, Carrie wants to help a rehab clinic whose staffing needs she had previously not been able to support. She watched for opportunities to reduce her button-pushing workload to a level that allowed her to step back and think more strategically about how she could help a more diverse client base.

Optmyzr's Campaign Automator let Carrie automate the creation of highly targeted ads based on job openings at her clients' companies. Next, she added Optmyzr's prebuilt scripts for budget pacing to control how much budget should be spent for all the different types of jobs and automatically make corrections to the allocation following days when she came in under budget.

Carrie was now able to pace the number of leads for each client at the optimal rate. She freed up an enormous amount of the time she'd previously spent pushing buttons. Her automations executed her strategies more efficiently and reliably than if she were doing it all manually. She could now do more of the strategic work she enjoyed and excelled at.

Layering in audience-interest signals, Carrie improved the quality of the leads by categorizing types of job vacancies and mapping them to interests desirable candidates were most likely to have.

Campaign Automator allowed Carrie to create more specific ads about the type of jobs she currently had available and show them to the types of users most likely to be great candidates for the open roles she was trying to fill. Because this strategy allowed her to handle her ad spend more efficiently, she was able to place higher bids where appropriate. Spending more for each click gave her an edge over even her largest competitors, who were buying leads and clicks generically.

Layering in just a few third-party automation layers had enormous downstream benefits for Carrie, her company, and their clients. These were exactly the mutually beneficial connections that Carrie had gone into her field hoping to make.

Please note that, just as this book uses Google Ads as a representative of many other ad systems, such as Microsoft's, so too will Optmyzr's off-the-shelf automation-layering tools stand in for all such third-party options. Optmyzr's tools are those I know best and believe in most. But several other companies have built comparable automations.

These tools simplify previously complex tasks and enable others previously unachievable. A company like Adidas, whether they have hundreds or thousands of products, could take days to manually structure the right campaigns for the right products. Automation layers allow them to specify templates for campaign structures just once, and have the machine build and maintain the resulting structure, a tremendous time saving.

Advertisers deploying automation layering are able to do search-terms analysis with more nuance, for instance, by using multiple date ranges. The automation layers proved to be an excellent means of spotting anomalies.

Google's comparison tool lets advertisers look for a query that had more than an $80 CPA over the last month, week, or day—but only over a single range of days. It can show that the $80 query cost $40 last week, but the only way to discover if it doubled in the previous week is to check that week.

There's no way to ask directly which prices doubled in seven days. That "running shoes" cost $80 per acquisition last week is much less interesting than knowing it was $40 the week before and $20 the week before that. There's clearly something worth investigating here.

Or course, even if "running shoes" is twice as expensive this week as it was last, $80 may still be a relatively inexpensive search compared with "sneakers," and well within the range of what an advertiser is willing to pay. On the other hand, if "running shoes" continues to double week after week, it could easily become too expensive. Without a tool watching for relative increases, the advertiser might end up paying over $1,000 per acquisition in less than five weeks.

Worse still, they will have lost the chance to respond in a timely manner to the rising cost of "running shoes" and its underlying causes. If five weeks of doubling acquisition costs were caused, for instance, by the entrance of a new competitor in the ads auction that they didn't know about, its inaction puts it at a disadvantage. If, on the other hand, they have an automation layer in place that is watching for exactly this kind of anomaly, they can update messaging to keep a new upstart from building up its quality score and poaching some of their impression share.

API

Leveraging the Google Ads API (application programming interface) lies on the far end of the spectrum of implementation strategies. This route is much more technically challenging and will probably require hiring a costly engineering staff. They'll need to build and maintain their own system and infrastructure, keeping it up to date with the Google Ads system's moving target.

Clearly, the three solutions presented so far are simpler and less expensive. However, for some edge-case companies, using a custom-made API makes sense.

For instance, some enterprises spend hundreds of millions a

year on Google Ads. An engineering team that builds out and maintains automation layers custom-tailored to their needs and designed to augment their value proposition could be a great investment.

But it's not a cost-effective answer even for the majority of large international firms. In other words, chances are your company or client isn't an edge case.

On the other hand, some advertisers may turn to the API after they run into some of the limitations of the lower-cost scripts we just covered. For example, let's anticipate a day when Alonzo's Autos has grown into such a success, or cars have gotten so complicated, that he now has a catalog of over a million products and wants to go beyond hourly updates.

Scripts can't do that because they run at most once per hour. Though the new Google Ads version launched in 2021 is no longer limited to working with a maximum of a quarter-million entities such as keywords, there is still a thirty-minute execution limit, which can make it difficult to process all entities in very large accounts. But Alonzo can no longer dump all this inventory into a single Smart Shopping campaign, as he wants to add some structure based on his product categories or profit-margin data.

Most of the available solutions will fail because his accounts aren't structured exactly the way off-the-shelf scripts and tools expect. Or he hits limits of how many items he's allowed to manage without paying a big upcharge. Or the system runs into time-out issues. Alonzo might reasonably conclude he needs to suck it up and invest in establishing an in-house, customized solution that will interface with the Google Ads API.

This move isn't recommended, however, unless all other options and approaches prove impractical. It now occurs to Alonzo that every other large auto-parts dealer—in fact, almost every e-commerce company of comparable size—is trying to meet the same goal. And they don't all need to create their own solutions from scratch.

A third-party PPC company like Optmyzr, which works with a variety of these vendors, could build such a system according to Alonzo's specifications in far less time—days rather than weeks or months—than it could be built using the Google Ads API.

Alonzo's quite happy about this. What's more, the third party can handle dozens of technical details on an ongoing basis, making sure everything stays up and running and his ads stay in sync with his inventory and business goals, as well as making adjustments that Google's regular code changes necessitate.

Google Ads' declared purpose has been and remains to help advertisers reach the right audience with the right bid and the right message. While it has built some automations that manage the whole process—most notably Smart Shopping campaigns—most of its automations focus on one portion of the bidding-targeting-messaging triad.

But we should resist following Google's example of looking at each component in isolation. Sophisticated advertisers know how interrelated all their activities are. Sometimes, setting the right bid isn't really about the bid's cost. Viewed holistically, your business goals might be better served by letting automated bidding set the price while you maintain tighter control over targeting. Likewise, if you have the wrong message, you're never going to be able to set a bid right enough to fix it.

Google is perfectly willing to try bidding as best it can with the wrong message or for the wrong audience. But this doesn't work for its advertisers.

Google's tools don't operate in isolation. Understanding how each fits into the larger whole—their potential conflicts and interdependencies—is a significant part of our role as strategists. With a strong, holistic strategy buttressed by automation layering, drilling down into each of the three pillars—strategic targeting, bidding, and messaging—can reveal more opportunities to unlevel the playing field.

Let's first move on to ways that automation layering can be implemented to deal with strategic targeting: the right audience.

CHAPTER 10

• • • •

STRATEGIC TARGETING

In the early days of Google Ads, targeting took the form of trying to situate ourselves behind the user's eyeballs and intuit what the people we'd most like to reach—those ready to convert—would type into a search box. It was up to the advertiser to imagine everything such a user might search on.

In other words, the "right audience" piece of targeting, bidding, and messaging was still tightly focused on search and keywords. *What were they going to type into the box?* We made guess after guess—a practice that was both tedious and imprecise.

AUDIENCES AND AUTOMATION

Things had to change and did. Early on, Google began introducing automations to manage some of that conjecture for us. It relieved us of the need to guess every possible misspelling by introducing different match types.

Keywords were of primary importance, because what people entered into the search box was the only information we had about what they were looking for. At that point, Google didn't really care about audience demographics on the theory that it didn't matter whether the person who just searched "flower arrangements" was male or female, old or young. What mattered was that they were looking for a florist.

Later, demographics—age, gender, household income, etc.— were introduced, shifting the focus from just what they were searching for toward who was searching, and using this new data to refine the message. A man in his fifties and a girl in her teens who search "flower arrangements" might both need a florist. But if Google showed Bernard's ad featuring $100 bouquet of a dozen roses to both, it was unlikely to earn two clicks, let alone two sales. It served both Google's interests and Bernard's to match a twenty-dollar Mother's Day bouquet with a girl searching in May, and the more expensive roses with an older man in February.

With the advent of machine learning, Google got to know much more about users and began to group them by their interests and psychographics. Taking myself as an example, Google knows I visit websites about cars and spend time reading financial news. I became, with others who share my interests, part of associated affinity groups. Advertisers can then select from several hundred such groups and automatically have a more filtered audience to show their display ads to.

Google can now show an ad to everyone who matches the advertiser's selected interest criteria. If a local car-detailing company selects "auto enthusiasts" as an affinity audience target, I'll likely see their ads. I'm a prime candidate.

But my thirteen-year-old neighbor, who's a rabid car enthusiast and spends more time on car sites than I do, will be shown the same ad, even though his interest is purely theoretical. He loves cars, but he's too young to drive, doesn't own one, and even if he did, would be more likely to wash it himself than pay to have it cleaned.

The car detailing company would be better served by a simple automation layer that looks at the performance of its ads by demographics and issues a report comparing the number of conversions by age group and for men versus women. Google has all the necessary data and will make it available if you ask. But you have to know what to ask and where to look.

This kind of audience-focused automation layer can also protect an established demographic as a company reaches out for a new one. For example, Lululemon, another of the Bernard Agency's clients, began life as a women's brand, but at the moment, one of their fastest-growing market segments is men's apparel. Yes, I also love their stretchy pants.

Lululemon can easily target people interested in sports and fitness, but if it knows a woman is searching, it would likely show an ad for its sports bras. It doesn't want to show that ad to men. For them, the messaging will be radically different. Bernard and Lululemon need an automation layer to help manage the complexity that comes with having more audience-based signals than ever.

IN-MARKET AUDIENCES

One of Google's newer innovations, In-Market Audiences, takes grouping by interest area to a more actionable level by identifying those members of a group who are not only interested in a product or service but actively in the market. With In-Market Audiences, Google can see that, in addition to regularly reading about the latest sports cars and keeping up with developments in driverless car technology, I seem to be in the market for a new vehicle.

This is the wizardry of machine learning. Google can match the type of websites I visit and my real-time behavior to those of someone ready to buy a new car. It's a capacity that even five years ago would have seemed like science fiction.

Google offers two ways for advertisers to match these audiences to their campaign or ad group: targeting and observation. When advertisers elect to target an In-Market Audience, Google only shows their ads to people within that specified audience segment. An advertiser who sets up such an audience for observation is simply instructing Google to track its performance.

Here again, the addition of an automation layer allows advertisers to get more out of Google's AI. Rather than restricting the number of audiences you observe to the number you can personally monitor, a watch-and-cull automation can spot audiences that are underperforming and eliminate them.

CUSTOM AUDIENCES

As mentioned, Google will provide you with a ready-made list of several hundred demographic and psychographic categories. It's all the average advertiser needs. But there's an opportunity here to further unlevel the playing field by creating categories custom-tailored to your company. Advertisers today can build a fairly exact profile of a person who's ready to convert and show ads only to users who match that profile.

As an example, let's look at Deidre, who runs a travel agency specializing in family packages to Disneyland. She wants to set up a Custom Audience. She carefully thinks through what she believes to be the typical behavior patterns of the people most likely to make a several-thousand-dollar purchase. She knows her audience well and thinks the people she wants to target would probably, at some point, have done searches for "vacation in California," "what is the most fun theme park?" or "family vacations." They've probably also looked at websites like Travelocity and gone onto the Disney.com website or Disney Plus.

This is not to say a user has to have done all those searches to be part of Deidre's custom audience. Rather Google will use the searches to build a model. Machine learning, as we've seen, assigns scores and sets thresholds. In this instance, it scores every user against Deidre's criteria. When a potential customer hits above the threshold, the ML concludes that user is part of Deidre's custom audience—a person with a likely interest in taking their family to Disneyland—and displays her ad.

While Deidre uses machine learning to better target her ad, she knows better than to trust that ML will always get things right. She sets up a performance-monitoring automation layer to closely watch her conversion rates and CPAs. She also keeps up with trends in her market and updates her Custom Audience frequently to keep her ads tightly focused in ways that only her thorough, professional knowledge of her audience could come up with. For example, she frequently adds new

Disney movie titles to her custom audience, as it seems likely that fans of Disney movies might be more interested than the average person in a visit to Disneyland while vacationing in Southern California.

Likewise, Nelson, whose Nelson's Nissans car dealership set up separate campaigns for the service department and new and used cars in Chapter 4, might notice, well before Google, the impact the COVID pandemic has on the relative demand for minivans and pickup trucks. Google would probably figure it out eventually, but Nelson, out on the showroom floor every day, notices minivan sales are stagnant while truck sales are way up.

With their offices closed but their businesses still open, contractors were in the market for mobile offices that can do double duty. Nelson makes a new ad group and informs Google that searches for "mobile office" might convert in a way they never have before.

Around the spring of 2021, Nelson has another insight. He sees used cars selling for a huge premium due to a severe shortage in the supply chain and a renewed demand for vehicles from consumers flush with some extra cash from government subsidies during the pandemic. In addition to updating his ad messaging to let prospective used car buyers know that they may be better off buying a new vehicle, he also creates custom audiences to target ads to people on the verge of selling their car. With fierce competition for used cars, he wants to be top of mind to a person who's considering selling their car and is looking up its potential value online.

PLACEMENT TARGETING

On the theory that you have to meet your audience where it's at, placement targeting can be an important factor in how you get your ad in front of the right eyeballs. Because Google has made it functionally impossible for advertisers to issue a broad prohibition against showing their ads in places many would like to avoid—Russian and Polish websites, for instance, or web apps—automation layers must now watch for such placements and create instance-by-instance placement exclusions in real time.

These automation layers constantly look for indicators of placements the advertiser does not want, as, in our example, websites with specific domain extensions like .ru (Russia) and .pl (Poland) or for the signature that indicates an app placement. The moment the automation layer detects such placements, it copies the address and tailors the equivalent of a negative keyword—called a negative placement—that specifically eliminates it as a target for the company's ads.

A similar automation layer can protect companies from having their ads shown on YouTube next to controversial or objectionable content. With over 500 hours of new video added to YouTube every minute, not even Google can completely stay on top of quality—or decency.

Still, no advertiser wants their ads shown next to a hateful video. The solution here is to have the automation layer check for the ratio of thumbs-up to thumbs-down ratings. The automation doesn't know what's in the video, and no advertiser has the time to look, but the moment it earns the tenth thumbs-down or its ratio of negative-to-positive ratings drops below 5 percent, the automation layer can prohibit that video from ever showing your ad again by adding it as a negative placement.

And what happens when you exceed the maximum of 65,000 negative placements Google allows your account? You can refine your automation layer to update the negative placements with the most egregious ones every day. For example, determine which placements have high volume on weekends as opposed to weekdays, and then start the 65,000 negative placements with the highest weekend volume around midnight Saturday and revert to the weekday negative placements around midnight Monday.

TARGETING STRATEGIES

The most effective targeting is obviously strategic rather than catch-as-catch-can. By reducing the need for tactical button-pushing, automation layering can, as we've seen, free up your time to do more meaningful strategic analysis.

The number of such strategic interventions is limited only by your own analytic and imaginative resources. The following set of targeting automation layers is not meant to be exhaustive by any means. Rather, it's a set of examples you may want to implement that's also meant to give you a sense of what's possible.

SHOPPING CAMPAIGNS

Should you run an AI-based Smart Shopping campaign or a conventional one? There are pros and cons to each option. Which to choose? As Eric Schmidt, Google's CEO at the time I worked there, would say in product meetings when asked to choose between two good options: why not do both? As long as you wear your PPC doctor hat and know the nuances of each, you very well can run Smart and regular shopping campaigns simultaneously.

Research makes it clear that if you do a single regular shopping campaign with a single ad group, it's going to do worse than a Smart Shopping campaign. If you don't have the resources to create more granular campaigns, stick with AI-driven Smart Shopping.

With regular shopping campaigns, you, as a power user, can set priorities. For example, you can put your best sellers in a high-priority campaign, so that for more generic searches only your best-selling products will show. If someone searches for "running sneaker," for example, the ad in first position will be the high-end Ultraboost.

To take a more complicated and representative example, let's say that Jim's bathroom fixtures business has a number of high-margin, claw-footed bathtubs in the warehouse that it would like to promote. Other bathtubs are drop-shipped and have lower margins.

The most logical approach would be for Jim to put claw-footed tubs in a high-priority regular shopping campaign, and all other tubs in a Smart Shopping campaign. The problem is that Google always prioritizes Smart Shopping over regular shopping campaigns, even higher-priority ones. Which means that the less desirable tubs, from Jim's perspective, would always be shown first. That's the opposite of what was intended.

But, as usual, there's a workaround. You can regain control but have to do so methodically and on occasion counterintuitively.

The only way to show "claw-footed tubs" first is to create a high-priority manual campaign for those products. Then put all other tubs in a low-priority campaign. Finally, put all of Jim's products *except tubs*—for instance, faucets, showers, and so on—into a Smart Shopping campaign.

When a user types in "tubs" or "bathtubs," Google Ads will recognize that nothing in the Smart Shopping campaign matches that keyword. So, it will default to the high-priority manual campaign, showing claw-footed tubs first, and only show the other bathtubs that will be drop-shipped if it can't make a match with the high-priority campaign. This strategy is by no means obvious, but it works.

KEYWORD TARGETING AND HIDDEN SEARCH TERMS

As we've discussed, Google is now showing fewer search terms in its reports. This is data to which you formerly had but no longer have access. But Google isn't the only game in town: a competitor such as Microsoft Ads, or an SEO tool that generates keywords, probably uses similar machine-learning technology to decide which search terms are relevant to a particular keyword.

The suggestion here is to find another system that has a tool that gives you suggestions as to what other keywords might be relevant to the base keyword you enter. It's fair to assume that those are probably search terms that Google might also consider using for your account.

Going through this assembly of search terms carefully, you can then determine which ones you want to make positive and which negative. Let's look at a case where that decision could go either way, depending on the circumstances.

Say you're advertising on the keyword "Rolex watches." A search query for "luxury watches" might be a good match. If that's the case, add it to your campaign and actively target it. After all, you may be selling Philippe Patek as well.

If you're only selling Rolex watches, however, "luxury watches" might not be a good fit, especially if you have a limited budget that you're already spending entirely on more closely related searches that include the Rolex brand name. Make "luxury watches" a negative exact-match keyword, because it doesn't really say "Rolex," and that's what you want to focus on.

By the way, notice you wouldn't want to add a negative broad-match keyword, "-luxury watches," because that would prevent your ad from showing for searches like "luxury watches from Rolex." By using the exact-match negative, you're telling the system to not show your ad when the user searches for just "luxury watches" and nothing more.

As of this writing, tools like Optmyzr or Google Analytics actually yield more search-term data than Google Ads. Another tip, then, is to check these tools to help with your positive and negative keyword targeting.

TARGETING PRIORITIZATION

Not all sales are created equal, and your targeting should reflect that. Say you make two sales, each totaling $100. To Google, it looks like you got two equally good conversions. But what if you layered in insights from your business to understand one of those conversions came from someone in Portland, where your typical customer has a higher lifetime value (LTV), and the other from San Jose, where typical lifetime value is lower?

Despite the identical sales figures, the former conversion and customer are clearly more valuable. Certain geographical locations are also more valuable than others. The same is true across a spectrum of parameters: you may decide that a conversion on a laptop is more valuable than one on a smartphone, or that an iPhone conversion is more valuable than one coming on an Android.

Automations are only as good as the information we share with them. Google provides the means to do so with its offline conversion imports (OCI) feature, discussed previously in Chapter 6. OCI allows you to feed additional information to the Google Ads system, beginning with tracking offline as well as online conversions.

As previously discussed, the mechanism for doing this involves associating the Google-generated GCLID (Google click identifier) with offline conversions in your own system, such as a CRM, and then importing the combined data back into Google so they can tell which clicks, and associated attributes, led to the best conversions.

Because Google understands the tremendous benefits of OCI for advertisers using automated bidding, they are working to lower the barriers to adoption. They will make it easier for advertisers who can't capture a GCLID to benefit from OCI, for example, by letting advertisers share an email address rather than a click ID with Google. This is a perfect example of automation layering: advertisers can build and maintain a relatively simple system to feed email addresses and corresponding conversions to Google, while Google uses its ML prowess to match those email addresses to the right clicks. And with over two trillion searches per year, that's no easy feat.

The Google Ads power user can also use conversion value adjustments, a native capability of the Google Ads system, to adjust conversion values. It works by transmitting a transaction ID in the conversion tracking code at the time of the initial conversion, like one captured on the thank-you page following a form submission or a cart checkout. Later, when you know more about that initial conversion, you can update its value by sending Google the new value and original transaction ID.

For instance, you could boost the data from Portland, telling the system that it is worth $105, while the San Jose conversion holds steady at $100. This basically tells Google that all else being equal, it should prioritize sales from Portland.

A retailer meanwhile could use the same conversion value adjustment to let Google know that part of an order was returned for a refund and that a $100 sale was in reality only a $70 sale. Whereas another $100 sale had no returns and was truly a $100 conversion. With that extra knowledge, Google's machine learning can help the advertiser find more desirable customers who tend not to make returns.

What's going to end up happening is that Google will automatically start to prioritize conversions from the Portland market or sales to customers who keep most of what they order. Now Google's algorithms know your preference and will try to get you more of the conversions you prefer. Same budget, higher quality conversions!

And as a preview of coming attractions, a Google conversion-rules tool is in beta as of this writing. This should facilitate the targeting-prioritization process considerably.

FEDERATED LEARNING OF COHORTS (FLOC)

What's FLoC or Federated Learning of Cohorts? Although we discussed this in Chapter 2, let's dig a little deeper.

By the time this book is printed, FLoC may either be the new technology that enables audience targeting, such as "in-market audiences," "affinity audiences," and others that had previously relied on data about individuals collected through third-party data collection with cookies strewn across the web, or it may be a technology proposal that died an early death. Regardless, a good perspective on this recent Google innovation stems from the second of the three truths: advertisers will have less access to data going forward.

As we've seen, this is largely due to privacy concerns and the ongoing prohibition of third-party cookies. Firefox and Safari already don't allow them. The technology that advertisers have depended on to do much of their audience targeting is simply not working anymore on a large number of browsers. In time, Google Chrome, the most popular browser, will follow suit.

Google has a big stake in this trend, both as the provider of the Chrome browser and the biggest PPC ad platform. It wants to make sure that some of these audience-targeting techniques continue to work, and it's working proactively to find solutions to these challenges. FLoC is its current cutting-edge response.

Google proposes establishing targetable cohorts based on certain interests, such as those looking to buy a new SUV. Advertising can then be targeted to these groups or cohorts without the use of third-party cookies.

The mechanism for grouping users into these anonymous cohorts is a public open-source algorithm that you can read more about at privacysandbox.com. An advertiser could now find out the cohort of a user visiting their site by adding one line of code on their webpage. Then prior to launching a campaign, they can already measure the performance of users in various cohorts.

Once they have some cohort-performance data, they can go into Google Ads and target the cohorts they identified as likely to convert. This is revolutionary because until now advertisers couldn't get data about the performance of a targetable group of users until they made the investment to target those users. Now they can get the data before doing the targeting, potentially saving thousands in wasteful experiments.

This multiplies the advertiser's scale, because the ad network can find all the users in the cohort and start targeting them. This despite the fact that the advertiser's data is based on a much smaller sample than the cohorts Google has created. So, while the advertiser may decide that a cohort looks desirable from ten organic site visits associated with browsers in that cohort, when they go to Google Ads to target that cohort, their ad can be shown to tens of thousands of other browsers in the cohort who had not found the advertiser's site organically.

How cohorts will be built is still being debated. At the time of writing, Google creates them based on what websites individuals have visited in the past week.

The way most advertisers will target their ads will remain largely the same. If you're interested in people in the market for buying a new SUV, those who have visited SUV pages in automotive websites over the last week would naturally be part of that cohort.

This may be a little bit less precise than the current third-party-cookie system, but it will still work well enough. On the positive side, FLoC also opens up some interesting new possibilities well worth discussing.

One thing advertisers can do is request the cohort of any user on their site, even if they didn't click an ad to get there. They can then start to build a more granular picture of the behaviors of the different cohorts, such as which ones tend to fill out the contact form and which ones don't. And even before advertisers spend a penny on online ads, they can know which cohorts are valuable prospects. Armed with that knowledge, they can target audiences with increasing accuracy when they're ready to start spending on online ads.

This is only one of many possible approaches. Looking at your organic and social-media traffic, you will develop an understanding of which cohorts should be targeted. Then you'll let Google know those are the cohorts you want to prioritize.

This wasn't possible before the introduction of FLoC. Just make sure that you update your website with the JavaScript code that requests cohort IDs from browsers. Then attach that cohort ID to the data you've been collecting, so that you can analyze it to determine the cohorts you want to target. It's likely your data analytics tools will help with this, but even if they don't, the FLoC technology makes it possible to do this on your own.

OPTIMIZED TARGETING

Google started shifting campaigns using audience expansion to a new automation called optimized targeting in summer 2021. This feature reminds me of the FLoC idea described above, where we start with identifying desirable user behavior and turn that into targeting ideas.

Optimized targeting automatically shows ads to people who are likely to convert. So, how's this different from audience expansion, which has been around since 2019 and works for a broader set of campaigns?

Audience expansion looks for similar audiences to show ads to more users. An advertiser who's selected the audience of in-market SUV buyers may see their audience expand to in-market car buyers because there is a similarity between these audiences.

Think of audience expansion as a system that starts from an advertiser's selected inputs and expands from there. That works fine if the advertiser has done a good job selecting audiences. But it won't capture new sales from entirely different audiences advertisers may have overlooked because they seemed too dissimilar for audience expansion to even try.

Optimized targeting on the other hand starts not from an advertiser's targeting settings, but from the results they report. When an advertiser gets conversions, Google analyzes attributes of the converting users. If they find a pattern, like what types of searches many converting users recently did, then the system will automatically start to show ads to other users with similar behaviors.

This is another example of the huge shift in how PPC is optimized. Rather than managing details like targeting, Google wants us to optimize how we teach their machines to do their job better, in this case by reporting conversions more accurately using systems like offline conversion tracking, value adjustments, or value rules, all of which have been covered above.

GEOGRAPHIC ANOMALIES

Geographic targeting has always been a PPC fundamental. It's even more so in a post-COVID world, where things are less homogenous than before. If you're in a major city, you'll be able to find a Starbucks or a Best Buy. Some locations may have curbside pickup only, while others are open for in-store business. But you don't want to invite someone to make Starbucks their "third place," or office away from the office, if the front door is locked.

Of course, there are an unlimited number of reasons why certain geographic locations may be underperforming. What's most critical is to be informed of where problems may have arisen, so you can take corrective action.

Optmyzr has developed a free script called the Geo Anomaly Detector that uses several weeks of historical data to calculate the average performance for each combination of day of week and location where ads are displayed. It then compares this average (the "normal") to yesterday's performance. When the difference exceeds an advertiser-defined threshold, it sends an email alert.

For instance, your ad may have gotten an average of 5,000 clicks the previous couple of Thursdays in Chicagoland but only 500 yesterday, which was also a Thursday. Or the metrics for the entire UK may be a bit off. You can only take action if you are aware of the problem, and the script will flag these discrepancies for you. Then you'll have to analyze why this happened. Perhaps there's news about the latest Brexit wrinkle that's depressed sales. You can then respond by lowering bids for as long as this effect persists.

REMOVING CONSTRAINTS

In the early, less automated days of PPC, targeting was largely defined by constraints: target these zip codes and females over forty. Part of the reason for this was to maintain tight control in a new and unfamiliar context.

Today, with the deployment of machine learning, it's time to take another look at these historical constraints. This involves a changing mindset and the realization that the only constraint that really counts is our goal. For instance, we'll take any conversion so long as it costs less than $25.

Once you make that shift, what you've done at first is add another constraint—the $25 CPA goal—to the others you already established. At this point it's not only possible but desirable to remove some of those earlier constraints.

Don't do this all at once, but a little at a time. Say you targeted certain zip codes because you determined that's where most of your customers and potential customers resided. Now with Google automation, you can loosen that. People outside of those zip codes might convert at lower levels than those inside them, but some that you would otherwise not have targeted will in fact convert.

You could just bid less for those, as long as the conversions fall within the $25 CPA goal. All of a sudden you get more volume.

Then you can look at keyword constraints. You probably used to have specific, exact-match keywords for precision. Google AI now invites you to let that go and let it figure out how closely related what someone typed into the search field is to your keywords. If something is related, but not closely, again the bid can be lowered. And your conversion volume will increase once again.

The bottom line is that as you make the leap into automation, you can slowly remove your historical constraints because the system may be able to find more volume and opportunity if you have fewer of them. This is illustrated by the following graphic:

Traditional Constraints Can Restrict Volume of Smart Bidding

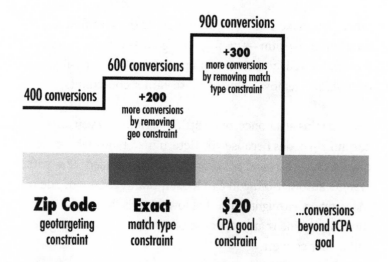

900 conversions

600 conversions

+300
more conversions
by removing match
type constraint

400 conversions

+200
more conversions
by removing
geo constraint

Zip Code	**Exact**	**$20**	...conversions
geotargeting	match type	CPA goal	beyond tCPA
constraint	constraint	constraint	goal

The next step in the process is monitoring what Google thinks is relevant to your business with a watch-and-cull mindset. You may look at a query and realize that even if Google gets a conversion here or there, it's so far from what you actually offer that it's probably an anomaly. Google AI may figure that out eventually, but you've done so much sooner. Then you can make that query a negative keyword, because you don't want to keep spending money until Google realizes that those searches are hardly ever going to convert.

Say, for example, you are an advertiser who sells cryptocurrency. All of a sudden, nonfungible tokens (NFTs) emerge. Google may think that this relates to your blockchain-related keywords, but you don't deal in NFTs. So, make "NFT" a negative keyword.

At the end of the day, you start peeling off the old constraints of your campaigns one at a time and monitor the resulting performance so you can add new, more relevant constraints instead. Keep doing this until you are spending all your budget, however much, within your own cost-per-acquisition or return-on-ad-spend limits.

These are some illustrative examples of targeting strategies and their implementation. As mentioned, these could be multiplied by using your and your team's and advisors' analytical powers, intuition, imagination, and intellect. Now you can put and keep the CPC strategist hat on your head.

Now, you're targeting the right audience. Next, let's take a closer look at the right bid.

CHAPTER 11

•

•

◉

•

STRATEGIC BIDDING

Smart Bidding was introduced in 2016—an age ago in PPC time but recently enough that many PPC professionals still find it something of a mystery. And while few would argue that manual bidding is better than automated bidding, there's much debate over which form of automated bidding to use. Should you use Smart Bidding or not?

The answer is "yes." Use Smart Bidding when appropriate and other forms of automated bidding, such as "maximize clicks" or "maximize conversions," when they're appropriate.

Automation layers and negative keywords can go a long way toward returning control to the advertiser, but they don't offer the option of returning to the days when all bids were set manually. Because of broad match keywords, close variants, optimized targeting, and other innovations, going forward there will always be a degree of fuzziness around when a specific ad shows up.

Consequently, it no longer makes sense to keep a single set

of locked-in static bids, or even bids that were automatically set but then persist for all searches until a new automated bid is calculated several minutes later. PPC is a real-time game and that requires intelligent use of real-time bids, like those Smart Bidding affords.

The top players in the finance world worry about how to get their servers a few miles closer to those of the exchanges, all for the sake of shaving milliseconds off their decision-making process and to get their orders processed faster than those of the competition. The least we can do in PPC is to similarly acknowledge that there is no justifiable reason to have stale (manual) bids for our ads. Google's automated bidding attempts to help advertisers adjust bids to the real world, where there is a more dynamic and nuanced relationship between message and audience.

PROS AND CONS

Google Ads is and has always been a cost-per-click system. The advertiser has the option to prioritize CPA (cost per acquisition) for services or ROAS (return on ad spend) for goods. Either way, the underlying process is the same: Google determines how much to bid on any given search by predicting which CPC (cost per click) best meets this goal.

Critically, the advertiser has primarily those two choices of tCPA or tROAS, neither of which are actual business goals. At the same time, investors never talk about ad costs. They talk about revenue growth and profit.

The average advertiser may be content to accept Google's goals as their own. To unlevel the playing field, however, you need to speak Googlese to Google. To set a ROAS or CPA goal, you reverse-engineer it from profitability goals.

It would be excruciating to do this manually for every bid you set, so an automation layer is needed. It can do calculations based on your real business goals, in the context of industry conditions and current consumer interest, to determine what good ROAS or CPA goals would be.

As an example of this, let's return to Deidre's travel agency. In addition to family packages to Disneyland, she also sells cruises, flights, and hotels. If her business goal is to maximize her company's revenue, she might determine she has a tROAS of 200 percent, that is, of doubling her investment. For every dollar she spends on advertising, she wants to get two in sales, and she sets that goal as her tROAS in automated bidding.

Google sees that cruises are very profitable for Deidre. Every dollar she spends on advertising cruises brings in ten dollars in sales. Air travel, on the other hand, is extremely competitive. Each dollar spent on ads for flights generates only a dollar in sales. But this isn't ultimately a problem since cruises more than offset the shortfall. She can afford to waste money on flights. Because her business goal is to maximize revenue, she's done the right thing.

If, on the other hand, her goal was to drive the most profit, she would need to find a way to separate cruises from flights so that the profitable category wasn't subsidizing the unprofitable one. She needs to make flights profitable on their own, either by setting a separate target that leads to better bids or by changing how much she gets compensated by the airlines for every seat she fills. Which isn't a bid-management issue.

The following charts illustrate reverse-engineering profitability from tROAS:

How Target ROAS Impacts Business Metrics

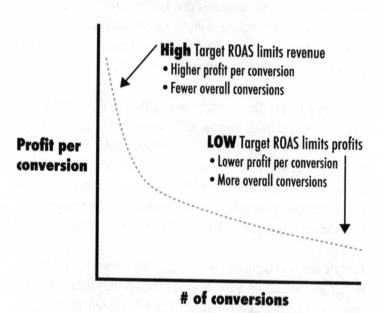

High Target ROAS limits revenue
- Higher profit per conversion
- Fewer overall conversions

Profit per conversion

LOW Target ROAS limits profits
- Lower profit per conversion
- More overall conversions

# of conversions

What tROAS Maximizes Profits

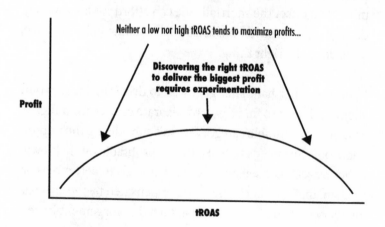

Neither a low nor high tROAS tends to maximize profits...

Discovering the right tROAS to deliver the biggest profit requires experimentation

Profit

tROAS

With an automation layer connecting her actual business goals to the intermediate goals Google allows her to set, Deidre can be confident it will try its best to make the right bids automatically. To receive maximum benefit, she'll use another automation layer to monitor performance and be very vigilant about responding to alerts.

In addition to linking your real business goals to the goals Google allows you to choose from, there are several other opportunities in bid management to unlevel the playing field with automation layers, many of which are of the monitor-and-alert variety. Before we get to a few of those, there's one very simple one that can be the difference between holding the field level and having it crater.

Bernard's agency has a new client, an up-and-coming online retailer of high-end hair products. One day, his bid management system notices the conversion rate has dropped dramatically. Doing its job, it thoughtfully reduces bids to protect him from wasting money on poorly performing ads.

Six months later, the company is no longer up-and-coming. It's going down fast. Bernard does some research and discovers the downward spiral started one day when the hair product company's landing page went down. The web team had it back up in under six hours, but by that time, the bid management system had essentially shut ads off, setting bids so low that they had stopped driving traffic to the site.

Smart Bidding's job is to set better bids by predicting conversion rates. But it entirely lacks the human professional's skills when it comes to explaining why a conversion rate might suddenly experience a dramatic change.

When conversion rates decline, even for a few hours, Google's bid management system will follow it down. Worse, because it has no way of knowing why conversions fell off, it doesn't know when the external cause that drove that fall has disappeared.

Bid management systems are self-propagating feedback loops, and a change in one direction causes more change in the same direction. If a campaign does badly, the system will exclude it, and that will make it do even worse. The ML systems have a bit of a confirmation bias, which is why we need to be more vigilant than ever as PPC practitioners.

A DOCTOR IN THE HOUSE

Understanding the cause of precipitous declines in conversion rates is something PPC marketers do as a part of their doctor role. But if they're unaware of the symptoms, they can't treat the cause.

Deidre, for example, might have such a monitor-and-notify automation layer in place. When it alerts her that performance has dropped sharply in New York but remains steady elsewhere, she can diagnose the cause—the New York Marathon was just canceled—and respond by adjusting her bids or launching a special promotion.

Deidre might also run into another bid-related issue that requires adroit handling. Say she decides to double her $10 CPA target bids on NYC hotel rooms to $20, because she expects to offset the higher cost per lead by doubling her conversion rate, because of a huge promotion she's planning to run on hotel rooms there. In effect, she knows she won't pay double the cost per lead and is instead just using the levers at her disposal to trick the system into getting her the most sales possible at her typical CPA target during a big promotion.

But Google will advise her against this sort of manipulation, even though it might well be the right move. Google tells advertisers not to change their targets for automated bids by more than 20 percent at a time or to make changes too frequently. Here again, an average user might rightly obey Google's instruction, but Deidre can confidently ignore it.

Deidre knows the reason behind Google's 20 percent rule has nothing to do with her business and everything to do with Google's. It's a lowest-common-denominator guideline. Google is worried that unsophisticated users, unable to properly contextualize their results, will think Smart Bidding is broken and stop using this especially useful automation.

When advertisers keep their targets within a fairly narrow range, their CPC stays relatively steady, because they're competing in similar auctions from one day to the next. Their ads play to roughly the same kind of user entering the same kinds of queries.

When an advertiser makes a change as dramatic as doubling their CPA, it can make them competitive for a class of query they previously didn't qualify for. Because Google doesn't have much data on the advertiser's performance in these new searches, it makes less informed predictions about conversion rates. Those guesses may be wrong. And if they are, the average advertiser, looking at campaign-level performance alone, will only see they doubled their CPA, and performance went down.

The savvy advertiser, however, does a deeper analysis. Rather than reading the campaign-level reports, they dig in and look at each individual ad group, keyword, or even query. More than likely, they'll find that the queries that worked well for them in the past have continued to perform, because Google has enough background on them to make accurate predictions.

However, the new, higher-quality queries for which the higher target has made them eligible may be much more erratic. Here, in a more detailed analysis, the advertiser may discover some big winners. But where they find new keywords that, in their judgment for whatever reason, are unlikely to ever perform well, they create negative keywords. The PPC doctor has fixed what ailed the campaign.

BIDDING STRATEGIES

The question remains: when should you rely on Smart Bidding AI and when should you supplement it with automation layers and other interventions? The answer varies on a case-by-case basis, and the best way to answer it is to give some specific strategic-bidding examples.

BUTTERFLY EFFECT

The term "butterfly effect" first appeared in chaos and complexity theory and refers to an effect disproportionate to its cause. A butterfly flapping its wings in Hawaii might be the first in a chain of events that causes a tornado in Iowa.

Optmyzr did a case study of an agency it works with that experimented with Smart Bidding in a few campaigns. Next thing they knew, their manual CPC campaigns blew up. A major competitor had reacted by changing *all* its bids, and this impacted all our customer's campaigns, regardless of bid strategy.

The takeaway here is to always be on the watch for the second-order effects of employing Smart Bidding. The best way to do this is to make sure that you have all the alerts discussed in the Measurement and Reporting chapter set up and that you're monitoring everything: not just what you think you're manipulating, but anything else that could be impacted through second-order effects.

ROAS MAY VARY

Let's start with a reminder: return on ad spend (ROAS) is not really a business goal. Profitability is. Items that have different margins should be assigned different ROAS targets in order to maximize profitability.

The counsel is to divide products into different categories based on profit margins. Make each category a separate campaign. To achieve profits, increase tROAS as the margin of a category decreases, as shown in the following graphic:

Campaigns by Profit Margin

	CAMPAIGN #1	CAMPAIGN #2	CAMPAIGN #3
PRODUCT CATEGORY	Lifestyle sneakers	Running shoes	Socks
CATEGORY MARGIN	High	Average	Low
CAMPAIGN GOAL	200% tROAS	400% tROAS	600% tROAS

Campaigns for products with lower margins need higher tROAS targets to be profitable.

In this simple example, we have five categories of products based on their margins, from highest to lowest. Your highest-margin products can be profitable at the lowest ROAS, and your lowest-margin products need a really high return on ad spend just to break even.

The key takeaway here is that, even if you're going to do automated Smart Bidding, you're not stuck with one goal. You can have multiple goals and set up multiple campaigns reflecting those goals. The system will use the same Smart Bidding algorithms but apply different parameters.

There's a caveat, however. Users don't always buy the exact product they initially clicked on. They might come to look at footwear, a high-margin product that has a tROAS of 200 percent.

But then they find some accessories like a pair of socks, which is a very low-margin product, and that's what they actually buy. Because the click came from the first, high-margin campaign, it's going to apply a tROAS of 200 percent to the low-margin purchase as well.

What needs to be done here is to determine what the cross-pollination between campaigns is for your business. What percentage of people coming in on campaign number one end up purchasing a product from campaign number five? That will help you arrive at a blended tROAS that accounts for people's actual behavior in the real world.

For example, let's say you know that a typical transaction including a flat screen TV, which has a 30 percent margin, includes about 10 percent worth of higher margin accessories like cables, which have a 50 percent margin. An advertiser could say that the margin on purchases on the flat screen campaign is (10% × 50%) + (90% × 30%) = 32%.

Another solution would be to fix conversion tracking to tell Google the true value of the conversions. Setting different ROAS targets to achieve profitability on products with different margins is a workaround for addressing incomplete conversion data.

Typically, advertisers communicate sales value or revenue in conversion tracking, even though they want to manage a campaign to profitability. As you may have guessed by now, advertisers can report their profit—revenue or cost of goods sold (COGS)—in the conversion value field and set a ROAS target of 100 percent to break even. If $1 of ad cost results in $1 of profit, not sales, then breakeven has been achieved.

IT'S ALL RELATIVE

Earlier in the book, I advised not striving for instant perfection when it comes to defining the value of conversions. Instead set relative weights of conversion values for microconversions, like white paper downloads or key-page views, that lead to the macroconversion of capturing a lead and closing a sale.

But if you follow the advice of using relative values rather than precise ones when you're using tROAS or tCPA, it's important to set reasonable target values that make sense for your vertical or industry. Machine learning doesn't think it's a great idea to buy $10 clicks when you report conversion values like $1, $2, or $3, and will throttle your volume. Google ML understands that bidding anything below 100 percent return on ad spend is inadvisable, since you're basically losing money.

Under most circumstances, it's not only possible but advisable to set relative rather than exact conversion values. If you set *relative* values of 100, 200, 300, you'll achieve the same prioritization without killing volume. It's as simple as determining the typical CPA in your industry and then not setting your microconversions at less than 50 percent of that level. If you're a lawyer expecting to pay $1,000 for a quality lead, then your lowest microconversion value should be set no lower than $500 in the Google conversion-settings screen.

Say you're a law firm that typically pays $100 per click, knowing that anyone who becomes a client will be a source of fairly substantial revenue. Don't then go to Google saying that when somebody fills out your lead-gen form and gets in touch with your firm, that the click was worth $10 or $20, because that's far less than what a click costs. At that point, the Smart Bidding system will figure that this isn't really a good investment of your money and will hold back on displaying your ads.

In this case, the firm would have been well advised to report that a conversion is worth $1,000, even if that's not the actual value, because this now serves as a benchmark. If what's defined as a conversion in this case is filling out a lead-gen form, you can then set relative values for a call to your office and then getting an actual client at $2,000 and $3,000, respectively. In another business, the relative value of registering for a webinar may be low, while downloading a pdf has a medium value and scheduling a demo a high one. It's not only possible but advisable under most circumstances to set relative rather than exact values.

The point here is not to get stuck on figuring out a conversion's actual value. Concern yourself with relative values, using those as a starting point, and then iterate from there. You can and should go back and adjust those values as appropriate, and eventually they will approach actual values.

This illustrates one of Google's principles of innovation, which is: don't let perfection get in the way of progress. Your business knowledge of the relative values of different types of conversion is a great starting point that can be further refined. But you can't refine it unless you start testing and iterating.

ADJUSTMENT DOS AND DON'TS

You can manipulate conversion values to help Smart Bidding do a better job for you. But there are certain adjustments you should make and others you shouldn't. Here's a list of the dos and don'ts.

Don't adjust values based on differences in:

- Expected conversion rates
- Typical average order values

Why not? You already communicate this to Google through your conversion data. Machine learning is already accounting and automatically adjusting for these factors.

Do adjust values based on:

- Lifetime value (LTV) expectations beyond ninety days
- Factors that Google doesn't acknowledge it considers, e.g., weather

With LTV, the cutoff point is ninety days because you can no longer restate conversion values in OCI (offline conversion imports) after that time. Whatever the value is at this point is locked within the system. But if you see that someone is going to become a high-value customer before that time, do adjust the conversion value upward.

Factors Google doesn't consider: remember Alonzo's Auto Parts and how his bids for batteries should have increased during the first cold snap of winter? Google doesn't publicly acknowledge and therefore Alonzo can't validate whether they actually look at the temperature to manipulate the bids for his battery campaign. It's up to you to determine where the system falls short and make adjustments.

But what if Google AI does take this factor into account, and you're just unaware of it? The worst-case scenario is that Google makes an adjustment, and you make an adjustment on top of that. Your adjustment may have become a bit too aggressive, but you can always dial that back based on your findings.

This is far less egregious than not making any adjustment at all. As they say at Google: don't let perfection get in the way of progress!

BEYOND RELATIVITY

Adjusting relative conversion values will significantly improve your Smart Bidding results. This is essentially a great first step, but only a partial solution. The next step is to report real conversion values.

The problem here is that often advertisers report the value of the total sale as the conversion value. But this figure is far less important than an indication of the sale's profitability, based on the profit margin.

The challenge is that you often don't know what the profitability was at the time of the sale. It's often easier to calculate profitability of a sale sometime afterwards, when the returns window has closed. At that point, you can make more accurate adjustments via OCI. This gives Smart Bidding much better data to operate from in refining its bidding strategies. The additional accuracy will always work to your advantage.

SMART BIDDING AND CAMPAIGN SIZE

At Optmyzr, we did an analysis of the difference of conversion rates (CvR) for manual and Smart Bidding across many different spend buckets. The following chart summarizes our findings:

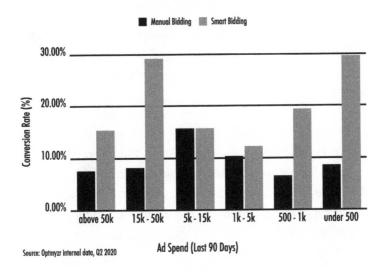

Difference in Conversion Rate (CvR) by Ad Spend

Source: Optmyzr internal data, Q2 2020

The first obvious conclusion to be drawn from this chart is that Smart Bidding does better than manual bidding in both large and small accounts, and not significantly better in mid-range accounts. Why?

Small accounts spending $1,000 or less over ninety days saw much better performance with Smart Bidding. These makes sense, because if you're an agency managing small accounts, you're probably not going to spend that much time on each of them individually. Automation will probably give you better results than manual bidding.

Moreover, small accounts often lack the depth of data able to support good manual bidding. Although machine learning also relies on such data, it's still able to help small accounts because their data includes thousands of signals that are not specific to the advertiser's account. Rather, they span industries and include general insights such as typical conversion rates based on device, browser, screen settings, and so much more.

Large accounts spending $15,000 and up over ninety days are also well-served by machine learning. This is because accounts of this kind generate large amounts of data, which is precisely what makes AI smarter.

Midrange accounts spending between $1,000 and $15,000 over ninety days show no advantage for Smart Bidding over manual bidding. These are often accounts you are developing and therefore paying a good deal of attention to. But they don't yet have a lot of data connected to them. Your understanding of context neutralizes the advantage of purely data-driven decisions made by the machines.

SEASONALITY

One power-user tip for keeping Smart Bidding in line is Google's seasonality bid adjustments, or, more simply, seasonality adjustments. This is an automation layer Google itself has put on top of Smart Bidding.

Say you're doing a special promotion, or perhaps there's a special event or holiday—like Arbor Day for a nursery—that only applies to your or your client's business. These adjustments override Smart Bidding's default. In setting this up you can say that you expect conversion rates to be, say, 50 percent higher in the next three days. During that period, Smart Bidding takes that adjustment into account in setting bids. The AI no longer needs to take the time it would have otherwise needed to figure this out.

At the end of the period, the seasonality adjustment automatically lapses. Smart Bidding knows that this period is anomalous, so they don't use the data to calculate future bids. Otherwise, the system might expect that adjustment to continue. Now, it reverts to the status quo after the designated period.

CONVERSION VALUE UPDATES

Conversion Value Updates, like OCI (offline conversion imports), enable you to update the conversion data that Smart Bidding takes into account. As previously discussed, OCI enables you to import offline conversions, often through a link between your CRM and the ads system, which Smart Bidding's system can then use to set better bids.

By contrast, Conversion Value Updates allow you to change

the value of a conversion already reported. If you get a return, the conversion can be entirely retracted. If there's a partial return, the value of the conversion can be restated. And if a customer's predicted LTV increases or decreases, due to parameters such as location or device type, conversions can be adjusted accordingly. Smart Bidding will then take the revised data into account.

The conversion value updates need to be done with a third-party PPC management tool, a custom API integration, or a spreadsheet template supplied by Google Ads. Once a conversion value is updated, it can't be updated a second time, so accuracy and care are required.

BID ADJUSTMENTS

In the days before Smart Bidding, bid adjustments helped set the right bid based on such common factors as geographical location, hour of day, day of week, and so on. However, bid adjustments don't work with Smart Bidding in Google Ads, though they do in Microsoft Ads. Yes, you heard that right.

The bottom line is that Google Smart Bidding will ignore most of your attempts to do bid management, as these factors are handled automatically. Only the system won't tell you that your adjustment hasn't taken effect, and you may very well mistakenly think you've accomplished something.

The following graphic shows where, as of this writing, bid adjustments are no longer viable, as well as where they still are:

	Strategy Name	Strategy Type	Device	Geo	Ad Schedule	Audience (incl. RLSA)	Demographics	Calls
Smart[3] (Real-Time Automated)	Maximize Conversions with tCPA	Conversions	✔ Adjusts target CPA[1]	✗	✗	✗[4]	✗	✗
	Maximize Conversions without tCPA	Conversions	minus 100% only	✗	✗	✗[4]	✗	✗
	Maximize Conversions Value with tROAS[2]	Conversions	minus 100% only	✗	✗	✗[4]	✗	✗
	Maximize Conversions Value without tROAS[2]	Conversions	minus 100% only	✗	✗	✗[4]	✗	✗
	Enhanced CPC[5]	Conversions	✔	✔	✔	✔	✔	✔
Automated	Maximize Clicks	Clicks	✔	✔	✔	✔	✔	✔
	Target Impression Share	Impressions	minus 100% only	✗	✗	✗	✗	✗
Manual	CPC	Clicks	✔	✔	✔	✔	✔	✔
	vCPM/CPM	Impressions	✔	✔	✔	✔	✔	✔

Bid Adjustment and Bid Strategy compatibility chart for Google Ads (August 2021) - www.optmyzr.com · **ØPTMYZR**

✗ Bid adjustments can be set but will be ignored.
✔ Bid adjustments can be set and will be used.

Yes, device and audience factors can be adjusted to a certain degree. But most factors cannot.

The advice here is simply to cancel any bid adjustments that are incompatible with your preferred bidding method. This will lessen confusion among your team members, who may think that something has changed when in reality it hasn't. Use conversion value adjustments, just discussed, instead.

Keep in mind that moving between different versions of automated bidding can make sense in some scenarios—for example, for campaigns that fluctuate between high and low conversion volumes, like seasonal campaigns. During the low season, when there isn't much conversion data, it may be better to maintain higher bids manually. Then, when the products become in-season and conversion volume returns, switch back to Smart Bidding to take full advantage of Google machine learning.

For these types of campaigns, removing bid adjustments makes less sense. Make sure your whole team understands when these adjustments do or don't apply.

Now that we've covered getting the right audience with the right bid, let's move on to the right message.

CHAPTER 12

·

·

·

·

STRATEGIC MESSAGING

In the days when PPC advertisers defined exactly which key-words would trigger their ad, they used to write a handful of variations on that ad that Google could choose from. Since, at the time, Google AdWords had limited ability to target particular audiences, ads for broad keywords were necessarily generic.

A broad keyword aimed at a broad audience can't, by definition, be focused. Earlier, I used the example of the keyword "hotel" to illustrate this point. "Hotel," like "sneakers," is a keyword that has its place. Early on, when Google couldn't filter audiences enough to know whether the user searching "hotel" was shopping five-star or budget, an advertiser would have felt no need to provide Google with more than two or three general ads.

Now, with the explosion of data about individual users and cohorts, the ability and desire to customize a message have increased dramatically. Google now asks advertisers to write up to fifty ad variants.

Google may be run by engineers, but it was smart enough about people to recognize how onerous this request was. And it engineered a solution—Responsive Search Ads (RSAs).

WHY RESPONSIVE SEARCH ADS

This automation collects an advertiser's headlines and product descriptions. It then assembles them in whatever way it deems best suited to the user who entered a relevant keyword. In the same way that advertisers can no longer be sure what broad variations of their chosen keywords might return an ad, they no longer know exactly what's going to be in an RSA.

The promise of Responsive Search Ads is that based on commonalities between users, the system can determine which message to deliver to whom. Previously, advertisers needed to create different ads for different audiences. For instance, Bernard needed one ad to show high-end Valentine's Day roses and another for inexpensive Mother's Day arrangements.

With Responsive Search Ads, Bernard would have listed both cases as different value propositions. Google showed the girl daisies and the older man roses. The RSA would have assembled, from Bernard's catalog of ad text components, information about happy mothers for the one, and wives (happy or angry) for the other.

Google can build both text-based RSAs and their display equivalent, which are called Responsive Display Ads. For the latter, the advertiser provides a logo, images, and a YouTube video, as well as text headlines and descriptions as usual. Google can lay out the ad to match the dimensions of whatever portion of a page it will occupy. It decides on the fly whether there's enough space to display the visual, or only the text and logo, and adapts accordingly.

CREATING RSA COMPONENTS

For Deidre's travel agency, the right message to get in front of someone shopping for a Disneyland vacation is likely to be kids meeting Mickey or on Splash Mountain. No text she can write will be as persuasive at reminding Mom and Dad of how much fun their own visits to Disneyland were when they were kids. Deidre can create a list of images and Google stands a good chance of getting the Mickey picture in front of the parents of young children and the roller coaster in front of the parents of teens.

Joe's Photo Shop is another good candidate for RSAs. Joe would need to provide fifteen headlines and four variations of description text that Google would then select from and combine in real time to create complete ads designed to be the best fit for each search.

This is potentially an extremely powerful automation. But Joe finds three components of the process challenging: generating the lists, measuring the performance of various permutations of each headline and description, and identifying and culling any underperformers. Here again, automation layers can capitalize on the power of Google's automations without burdening Joe with more to manage.

GENERATING LISTS

For Responsive Search Ads, every ad group needs its own list of up to fifteen headlines and four description variations. For the advertiser with hundreds or thousands of ad groups in their account, it's going to be both incredibly time-consuming and quite tedious to produce these lists of variations.

Joe's Photo Shop needs an automation layer that will comb through the last several years of his company's ads by product group, split out the headlines and descriptions, and use them to assemble his RSA lists. Optmyzr, for example, has an RSA-builder tool that can generate Responsive Search Ads for Joe's entire campaign in twenty-seven seconds (yes, we timed it)—much less time than it would take him to do the same for a single ad group using Google's interface.

EDITING HEADLINES

The RSA process expects advertisers to trust Google's judgment and leave its system to run the right headlines and discard any that underperform. Machine learning, once again, makes such decisions by assigning scores and setting a threshold. It rates how each headline performs and eliminates any with scores below the threshold.

This system is fine as far as it goes. But what if Joe wants to set his own thresholds? What if he's wasting several slots on his list of fifteen headlines because Google is simply not selecting them to show users? He certainly can't, nor would he want to, scour through every combination returned for each query.

An automation layer that "read" the Google reports field for "AdStrengthInfo" and made decisions about how to optimize the lists would help Joe understand which ad components commonly appear in ads with good ad strength and which in ads with ad strength problems. By doing this analysis across his whole account at once, he could get quick insights into which headline variations to try more of and which ones to scrap in favor of new ones.

MEASURING PERFORMANCE

Typically, advertisers only look at campaign-level or ad group-level performance. If Joe implements Responsive Search Ads and sees his conversion numbers improve, he's likely to think it's doing great and miss a tremendous opportunity to do better.

The improvements Joe sees are a campaign's averages. And averages often obscure important information. Joe could well have higher averages overall, despite the fact that some campaigns, unbeknownst to him, are tanking.

If Joe wants to check in and make adjustments on a more granular level, he'll need to analyze each query, checking each possible search term to see how it performs. This is a complex analysis that Joe needs to automate. And he also needs an automation layer that filters those campaigns that aren't performing as well as they could.

Armed with that information, Joe could make decisions based on his twenty years of experience in the camera business and deep knowledge of his customer base, rather than letting Google make those decisions for him.

RSA PROS AND CONS

RSAs have their critics. As discussed in several other contexts, advertisers see a disconnect between what matters to them—conversions—and how Google earns its income—cost per click regardless of outcome.

However, travel agent Deidre's RSAs might qualify for queries it previously didn't qualify for, just as they would if she doubled her tCPA. Formerly, if the Google AI determined that Deidre's ads were not relevant to certain queries, it wouldn't have shown her ads no matter how high she might have been willing to go with her bids. Now, because of the flexibility RSAs give Google to construct an ad based on what it determines will resonate with users, Deidre's ads rank high enough to be shown for some of those queries for which they previously didn't qualify.

For some of those new queries, Deidre's ads may indeed have lower conversion rates. But they're reaching new users. Even if conversion rates are very low, Deidre is still getting conversions she had no access to in the past.

At this point, the only question that remains is whether the conversions are too expensive. It's a critical question average advertisers rarely ask because, if they see their ad group's overall conversion rate fall with the implementation of RSAs, they reflexively turn the automation off.

Savvy advertisers won't spend their time doing such tedious, painstaking evaluation manually. They'll use an automation layer to do the extra work of digging below the overall conversion rate to understand on a granular level what's working and what isn't. They'll also periodically check the relative performance of their Responsive Search Ads' components. Afterward, they'll make appropriate adjustments.

As always, Google AI assigns scores and draws thresholds to generate your Responsive Search Ads. But you might not agree with all its assessments. To continue unleveling the playing field with Responsive Search Ads, savvy advertisers will monitor their performance. They'll take advantage of Google's combination reports, which show which headlines got the most impressions and how it put headlines and descriptions together.

Occasionally, in doing this, you'll catch a semantic anomaly where two well-targeted components combine to produce one that's clearly off target. Deidre, for example, might have a headline "It's easy to book," which, when paired with the description "Store your bags with our concierge," places the words "book" and "store" next to one another. Users read "book store" which, while not wrong, is certainly confusing.

These are the kind of glitches that the human eye immediately recognizes but which AI is blind to. The average advertiser doesn't go looking for them, but savvy ones do.

The bottom line is that RSAs must be doing something right. Three-quarters of advertisers use RSAs and find them useful. Only a minute number have stopped deploying them, as the following chart shows:

RSA Adoption

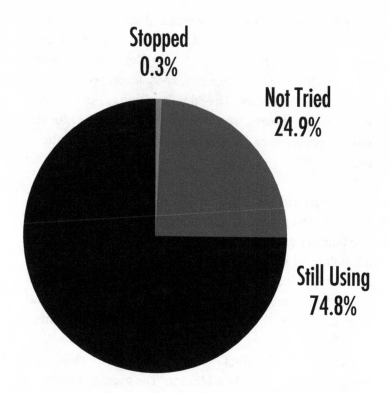

Stopped
0.3%

Not Tried
24.9%

Still Using
74.8%

Out of 4,200 accounts that tried RSAs, just 17 stopped using this automation.

Source: Optmyzr study 2020

WATCH OUT

The point, as always, is to keep a sharp lookout for content issues that might cause your campaign to underperform. Two common cases have to do with broken links and expired promotions.

BROKEN LINKS

One effective component of good messaging is the destination URL—clickable links that take a user from your ad directly to a specified page on your site. Large and even midsized advertisers can have hundreds to multiple thousands of such links, each of which, if broken, might cost you potential customers, not to mention the money you spent getting them to your site in the first place.

The problem can be solved with a URL checker, a tidying-up automation layer that watches for and notifies you of any page that doesn't return a 200 or "page okay" response code. Simple is effective.

EXPIRED PROMOTIONS

I know firsthand the frustration users experience when they respond to an ad featuring a sale or other promotion that is no longer current. In the first week of January, I saw an ad offering two-for-one Masterclass.com memberships.

I followed the link, ready to sign up. Unable to find the two-for-one option, I called customer service, only to learn that promotion had ended on New Year's Day. This isn't the way to create strong positive feelings in your potential customers! A small automation layer that looked for and culled outdated offers could have saved Masterclass and me from a negative experience.

MESSAGING STRATEGIES

Has AI taken over creative functions as well as important aspects of targeting and bidding? The answer is: not yet. And maybe never. While AI is making advances in the qualitative as well as quantitative sphere, it's impossible to know what the future will bring. As for the present: human PPC teachers are still the only ones capable of creating the most impactful ad messaging, text, and images. You can't automate creative. At least not yet.

But, as we've seen, machine learning has already entered the messaging and creative space. And what it can do will be done more effectively with automation layering. Here are some ideas to help unlevel the messaging playing field.

MORE RSA TIPS

As we've seen, RSAs are built up out of components. Fortunately, Google assigns scores to components and will share them with you via what they call "asset reporting." The component scores system is quite simple: poor, average, good, excellent. Any component scoring poor or average should be revised to bring its score up to good or excellent.

The goal is to find RSAs that have poor or average components in the headlines. However, if you have a big account, this might mean a lot of components. If that's the case, prioritize finding and working on poor ad components in ad groups with the most spend. Fixing those is going to give you the biggest bang for your buck across your whole account.

A simple script will help you find high-volume ads with one or more low-relevance headlines. Once rooted out, those components can be optimized.

Google lowers the score for your ads if they are too repetitive. Since you're not going to write exact duplicates of your headlines, the trick is finding headlines that are too similar to one another.

A good way of proceeding is to write a script that does an n-gram analysis of your headlines. Such an analysis simply counts the number of times you reuse words in a string of text, such as the text for all your headlines.

Take the following example of two headlines Bernard might use for his florist client:

- Buy nice flowers
- Purchase nice flowers

An n-gram of these headlines would be scored as follows:

- Flowers: 2
- Nice: 2
- Buy: 1
- Purchase: 1

Two words are repeated: nice and flowers. Since flowers is almost certainly a keyword, you don't want to eliminate repetitions there, because they boost relevance. But "nice" should be changed in at least one of your headlines. Come to think of it, probably in both.

How do you quickly get started with RSAs for a big account? Simply take your existing ad text components, including headlines, from your legacy Extended Text Ads (ETAs). Then move them over to the description and headline components of the RSA. There are scripts and automation-layer tools that will facilitate and shorten the entire process.

A warning: many advertisers report RSAs tend to have lower conversion rates than ETAs. When measuring efficacy, look at incremental gains.

The following chart shows the relative performance of RSAs and ETAs, based on an indexed Optmyzr survey of more than 5,000 accounts:

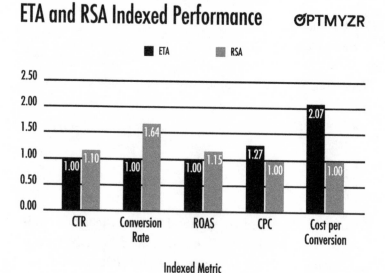

ETA and RSA Indexed Performance   ⊘PTMYZR

RSAs are clear winners in all metrics.

To dip your toe in the water, use the Drafts and Experiments framework to add RSAs to an existing campaign. Then measure results to see if the RSAs got more conversions, within acceptable tROAS or tCPA limits, than the ETAs. If so, the RSAs are helping you achieve real business goals.

Why should this be so? RSAs will be shown more often than ETAs, because of their relevance for additional search terms and a higher quality score.

MANAGING QUALITY SCORE (QS)

As previously mentioned, Google Ads' first real ML automation was the Quality Score (QS). It's a measure of relevance and is used in combination with CPC to determine the rank of ads in an auction. Its purpose is to show the right ad to the right user at the right time.

QS is the automation that picks an advertiser's most relevant ad to give it the best possible exposure to prospective clients. Thanks to RSAs, Quality Score has more flexibility to construct a relevant ad on the fly. But it's still limited by the headline and description variations you give it.

Hence our work in optimizing Quality Score includes:

- Being smarter about the ad components we feed into the system. This is the job of the human PPC teacher and has not been automated.
- Being exhaustive and complete in providing inputs for all ad extensions. (See below for more on these.)
- Keeping ad components in sync with the real world, including promotions and sales, and responding to what

competitors are doing that may impact messaging. This can be handled with an automation layer consisting of a script that updates your site links with sales or special promotions.

Wherever you find low Quality Score ad groups is where you should intervene and optimize the creative. If an ad group can't automatically show the right ad for the right user, that's going to be reflected as a low Quality Score in your account. A low Quality Score will point out where Google, despite its best efforts, hasn't been able to deliver, and assuming your keyword is relevant, you need to help it along by coming up with fresh variations of headlines and descriptions.

AD EXTENSIONS

Extensions are text snippets, apart from headlines and descriptions, that can be added to your ads to improve relevance. These can include: "deep linking" to specific pages on your website that may be particularly appropriate to an offer in your ad; location information, including locations of your affiliates; phone numbers and call buttons; callout text such as "free delivery" or "order now."

An RSA will only show ad extensions when they are deemed appropriate. The PPC teacher's job is to supply and update the extensions' text. Put this on your to-do list if you are serious about maximizing the impact of your ads.

AD CUSTOMIZERS

Ad Customizers are a way advertisers can templatize their ads and connect them with spreadsheet data. For the most part, the only "automation layer" you need in deploying Ad Customizers is to be a power user of tools already built into the Google Ads system.

Until fairly recently, these RSA components had to be fully written out, so they were basically static. Now, Google allows them to be customized automatically.

Examples of Ad Customizers are:

- Countdown timers
- Location insertion
- Business data

Looking at each of these in turn, let's start with countdown timers. These automatically update an ad during a sale or similar event. Today the ad will say "only seven days left" and tomorrow "only six days left." Or, if you want to create a sense of urgency, it could say "Get $400 off our newest exercise machine. Only five hours left!" I personally succumbed to this messaging and bought a Tempo home gym to stay in shape.

Locations can be inserted automatically depending on where the user is located like this: "Flowers delivered to {LOCA-TION(City)}." You could have a single ad that alternatively reads: "Flowers delivered to Los Altos" or "Flowers delivered to Mountain View," depending on the searcher's location.

A more advanced way to use ad customizers with location data is through a spreadsheet feed with different associated texts for different cities.

TARGET LOCATION	DISCOUNT (TEXT)
Los Altos, CA	$10
Mountain View, CA	$15

This requires all targeted locations to be included in the spreadsheet, but the extra work enables far more customized and relevant ads. Now, users can be shown different discounts depending on their location, which could be a country, a region, or a city. Different ads are shown to users in different locations without having to create many copies of the same campaign.

Sometimes this can be very practical, as with our previous example of letting users know if there are shoes in stock in stores, say, within a twenty-mile radius of where they're located. Sometimes, as in the text snippet "next day delivery in Poughkeepsie," the purpose is simply to personalize an ad in such a way that users will be inclined to gravitate toward it.

The final example, incorporating what Google calls business data, is more sophisticated, and its implementation requires an automation layer.

This can build on the location information just discussed. Say you determine that the most popular flower in Los Altos is roses, while in Mountain View it's tulips. Your spreadsheet will now have three columns: city, flower, and discount price. When there's an inquiry from Los Altos, the ad will now say "Get $10 off roses delivered to you in Los Altos." When the inquiry is from the next town over, the ad will say, "Get $15 off tulips delivered to you in Mountain View."

TARGET LOCATION	DISCOUNT (TEXT)	POPULAR FLOWER (TEXT)
Los Altos, CA	$10	roses
Mountain View, CA	$15	tulips

Your ad has become much more dynamic, speaking directly to users in specific locations. Similarly, you could offer different ads to someone who has already been to your website and someone who hasn't by using IF functions and connecting those with your first party audience lists. Perhaps you want to offer an introductory 10 percent discount to first-timers.

An automation layer could be used here to build and update the spreadsheets that feed this business data into the system. If orchids become more popular than roses in Los Altos one day, the system will now deliver an ad to a user in Los Altos featuring a discount on orchids.

SEARCH RESULTS PAGES (SERPS)

Earlier, I recommended using data sources besides Google's search terms report to get deeper insights into what users are typing into the search bar. You can likewise look beyond your own ads data to help craft the perfect marketing message.

Chris Konowal and Tracy McDonald of Seer, a digital agency, explain this technique as follows. Look at the organic and paid listings on search results pages (SERPs) for your most important keywords to better understand the typical user who types those words into the search.

Google's SERPs are finely tuned to give users the answers they need. To do so, they may suggest similar searches: "People also ask..." Or they may give a variety of types of answers, including images, videos, maps, and more. The ads from organic search results may themselves indicate typical user sentiment. Do they seem frustrated, happy, or neutral?

All this is marketing gold. The better you understand your prospect, the easier it is to give them a message that will resonate.

For example, the SERP for a search for "how to fix a leaky toilet" starts with several videos. Maybe your client should make a video of their own to have a chance at a top of the page of organic results.

Or if they don't want to wait for their own video to rank on this SERP, you could take a hint from Google and show a video on your client's landing page. After all, the reason Google shows more videos on some SERPs than others is because their ML has detected a user preference. So, if your keyword is correlated to users wanting to see videos, you can use that new insight to make your landing page better by including a video there, too.

Then the page suggests users also searched for "slow leaks" and use words like "running toilet." These provide ideas for RSA components, such as:

- We fix running toilets
- Stop a slow toilet leak
- Water leaking into the bowl

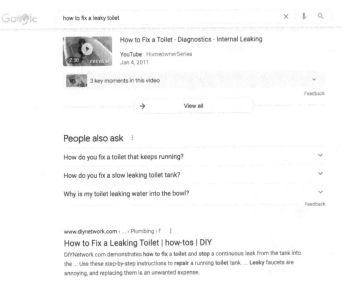

Next, Chris and Tracy notice the top-ranking domain is diy-network.com. This could indicate this search is dominated with DIY users who might not necessarily be looking to hire someone. This is a great way to adjust ad copy—for example, by including text like "Don't worry about trying to fix a leaking toilet yourself. Let the pros handle it!"

When you do these things, you're helping the machine become better. To do so in a more scalable way, consider an automation layer that analyzes hundreds of SERPs for you and puts the data in a spreadsheet where you can reverse engineer the right answers for particular users. The team at Seer did this, and they are thriving.

SHOPPING ADS

For shopping ads, you don't write ads the way you normally do in PPC. But, contrary to what many advertisers believe, this doesn't mean that you can't optimize your ad. You still have some control because this data, which includes the title, a product image, and the price, is already in your merchant feed.

First, you can optimize the title based on the product category. If users are shopping for apparel, they usually want to know the brand, gender, product type, and attributes like size and color. The recommended approach is to start your title with the brand, then the gender, and finally product attributes. For example: "Lacoste Men's Polo Shirt Size Medium Blue."

For special occasions, on the other hand, buyers care more about the occasion than the product type. They want to know if the product is a birthday card or a get-well card, but most care much less if the card's brand is Hallmark or Papyrus.

This can all be optimized by manipulating your Google merchant feed. One of the columns in your product data shared with Google is the product title. Simply edit this field for every product. To do this at scale and with an automation layer, you could use a tool that grabs the fields like brand, product type, and gender from other parts of your existing feed and then combines them in the right sequence for the template for each product category.

And just as you can optimize Smart Shopping campaigns by optimizing the merchant feed, you can optimize dynamic search ads (DSAs) by taking control over your web pages. Clearly, the role of PPC specialists now requires skillsets that are well out of the realm of managing just a Google Ads account.

The product image stands out in shopping ads, so photographs need to be carefully planned and executed. Many sportswear companies now have entire teams devoted to color research. Users looking for apparel are generally swiping quickly through a product-listing or Instagram page. A jarring or vivid color will make the user stop, look more closely, and maybe even buy. As rock-star PPC marketer Larry Kim puts it, you need to be a unicorn in a sea of donkeys, so your product stands out.

While the colors in the image should stand out, the titles should be standardized. To take an example at random, Gildan has a T-shirt in a color it calls Atlantis. To me, the color looks like the inside of a neon avocado.

Most people who might be interested would simply be looking for a green T-shirt, so that's how the description should read in the title. Instead of giving this product the title "Gildan men's T-shirt—Atlantis," call it "Gildan men's T-shirt—Green." While the user will simply see the color in the image of the ad, look at how much more prevalent a search is for "green T-shirts" than for "Atlantis T-shirts":

You can also maintain a promotions feed to further highlight your offer. Google found that from 2020 to 2021, searches for "deals" increased by 50 percent so if you have a deal, that's worth mentioning to prospective buyers. Most people think of extensions in the context of RSAs and ETAs. But Shopping Campaign Ad Extensions also include local inventory and promotions extensions. If you have a product in stock locally or are offering a discount, you should take advantage of these features to help your ad stand out from the rest.

We've now covered the three aspects of "the right audience at the right bid with the right message." Once again, the implementation tips here are illustrative. Many of you will find them useful, but there are many more ways to unlevel the playing field. But when all is said and done, ads still have to be written by humans to work well.

PART 3 SUMMARY

IMPLEMENTATION

By definition, implementation is where the rubber meets the road. It's where the digital marketer's work necessarily becomes granular, limited only by your strategic, analytic, and creative powers.

It all comes down to the fundamentals: reaching the right audience with the right bid and the right message.

The four basic, related approaches to strategic implementation are:

1. Become a power user of Google's built-in tools.
2. Use third-party scripts.
3. Use third-party automation tools.
4. Employ a development team to work with the Google API (Application Programming Interface).

While it's highly unlikely you'll need to use the last approach, it's more than likely you'll want to use the first three in tandem and as appropriate.

Strategic targeting comes down to finding or determining the right audience. There are several good options for doing so, and no reason not to combine them. For instance, you can combine Smart Shopping campaigns, which use AI to determine targeting, and regular shopping campaigns, utilizing your own demographic and psychographic analysis.

Smart Bidding is Google AI's premier **strategic bidding** innovation. Research shows that this is a great option for small and large accounts, while medium-sized accounts benefit from a more hands-on approach. Again, you can choose from both Column A and Column B as needed.

As a general rule of thumb, **don't** adjust bids based on differences in:

- Expected conversion rates
- Typical average order values

You've communicated these to Google through your conversion data, and machine learning is already accounting and automatically adjusting for these factors.

Do adjust bids based on:

- Lifetime value (LTV) expectations beyond ninety days
- Factors that Google doesn't acknowledge it considers, e.g., weather

At this point in time—and perhaps well into the future—

creative **strategic messaging** remains basically the domain of humans rather than AI. But that doesn't mean that the machine can't help you analyze what does and doesn't work creatively.

Responsive Search Ads are Google's primary, somewhat controversial foray into ML messaging. To continue unleveling the playing field with Responsive Search Ads, savvy advertisers will closely monitor their performance, with the aid of automation layering, and adjust accordingly. However, creating the right message for the right audience is ultimately up to you. Time for your "A" game.

CONCLUSION

In my first book, *Digital Marketing in an AI World*, I answered the question of whether human PPC professionals will continue to be essential to the automated Google Ads system with a resounding yes. The formula was:

HUMANS + MACHINES > MACHINES ALONE

In the two years since then, AI and machine learning have continued to evolve at dizzying speed. Google Ads and the comparable systems at Microsoft, Amazon, and elsewhere have become considerably more capable. Moore's Law tells us that this exponential speed of change will continue going forward.

This is why we are in the middle of the biggest mindshift in PPC history, as well as the three major challenges that we, as PPC professionals, now need to face and overcome:

1. Ad platforms will continue to automate.
2. Advertisers will have less access to data going forward.

3. Advertiser control over targeting, bidding, and message will keep decreasing.

Google ML automations, such as Smart Bidding, RSAs, Shopping Ads, and FLoC (Federated Learning of Cohorts) work perfectly well if you want average performance. Nobody wants that, but if you don't have the bandwidth to devote to optimization, it's probably best just to stick to the system.

But to both meet current challenges and unlevel the playing field, your expertise and intelligence are more critical than ever. Today, the formula has changed somewhat:

HUMANS + MACHINES > MACHINES ALONE
(assisted by smart automations)   (that run complex AI automations)

Taking on the strategist mindset, in addition to those of doctor, pilot, and teacher, PPC professionals can achieve superior results by tweaking the system through two related tactics:

- Becoming a Google Ads power user and taking advantage of built-in features that many don't even know exist; and
- Deploying "smart automations," that is, automation layers that enable the efficient incorporation of your unique business goals into an otherwise level playing field.

There are many ways that automation layers can be created and deployed. For those with a technical background, this might be DIY. However, there are also many third-party automation layers, such as Optmyzr's, you might want to consider deploying.

Of course, the fundamentals, including account structure,

measurement and reporting, and experimentation, continue to demand close attention. But in this new landscape, a new mindset is needed, one that looks for opportunities to leverage ML by integrating it with your or your client's specific business needs.

These requirements are focused on conversions and profitability, aiming:

- To reach the right customers with the right targeting
- For the right price with the right bid
- And with a more compelling message and the right creative.

Creation and implementation of automation layering strategies are limited only by your analytic skills and imagination. The more these human faculties are applied to your campaigns, the more you'll be able to rise above the competition.

RESOURCES

**Find Resources
Related to This Book At:**
https://www.optmyzr.com/books/unlevel/

OPTMYZR